AFTER EVEREST

AFTER EVEREST

Inside the private world of
EDMUND HILLARY

PAUL LITTLE

with Carolyne Meng-Yee

ALLEN&UNWIN
SYDNEY・MELBOURNE・AUCKLAND・LONDON

First published in Australia in 2012

Allen & Unwin
Sydney, Melbourne, Auckland, London

83 Alexander Street
Crows Nest NSW 2065
Australia
Phone: (61 2) 8425 0100
Email: info@allenandunwin.com
Web: www.allenandunwin.com

Level 3, 228 Queen Street
Auckland 1010
New Zealand
Phone: (64 9) 377 3800

A catalogue record for this book is available from
the National Library of New Zealand

ISBN 978 1 877505 20 1

Typeset in Adobe Caslon 12/17 pt by Midland Typesetters, Australia
Printed and bound in Australia by Griffin Press

10 9 8 7 6 5 4 3 2 1

CONTENTS

'You can't do that to me. I'm an icon.'
—Ed Hillary

'Well if you have a big life, a lot of stuff happens.
Dad had a big life.'
—Peter Hillary

ACKNOWLEDGEMENTS

One of the great pleasures of working on this book has been the opportunity it gave to meet and talk to some of the many remarkable individuals who touched or were touched by Ed's life. Our thanks for sharing their time and insights to:

Kevin Biggar, Pat Booth, Hilary Carlisle, John Claydon, Graeme Dingle, Mike Gill, Roger Goodman, Norman Hardie, Rebecca Hayman, John Hillary, Peter Hillary, Sarah Hillary, Alexa Johnston, Murray Jones, Naomi Lange, Mary Lowe, Ken Richardson, Mark Sainsbury, Tom Scott, Cath Tizard, Judith Tizard.

June Hillary was kind enough to consider our request but regrettably chose not to be involved with the project.

INTRODUCTION

When Ed Hillary descended from the summit of Mt Everest, the highest point on earth, on 29 May 1953, he was on his first day at a job no one had done before. Conqueror of Everest turned out to be a full-time career. Ed had to work out for himself what the job entailed and how to do it. In many ways, though he was a prodigious planner he spent much of the rest of his life making it up as he went along.

Many books have been written about the life of Sir Edmund Hillary, most of them by Ed himself. After each great adventure, he produced his own account; in all he wrote or co-wrote sixteen volumes. These include the autobiographies *Nothing Venture, Nothing Win* (1975) and *View from the Summit* (1999), as well as a memoir jointly authored with his son Peter in which they tell their own, sometimes overlapping, stories in half the book each; and Ed's accounts of various expeditions and adventures from Everest on. Many of those who went along on one of Ed's adventures penned their own account of it, sometimes in conjunction with Ed. These include not only Ed's first wife, Louise (three books) and son

Peter (ten books) but such friends and colleagues as Peter Mulgrew, Mike Gill and Desmond Doig, each of whose writing fills gaps in Ed's own accounts.

So when we told people we were writing this book, most expressed some doubt that the world needed another book about Ed. Then they would invariably add, after a pause, 'Though all that business with the family is interesting.' Similarly, when we approached people close to Ed and asked them to speak to us for this book, we could almost hear them silently saying to themselves at the other end of the phone: 'What—another one?'

We spoke to many people from Ed's immediate circle, nearly all of them impressive and charismatic individuals in their own right. Many said from the start they didn't want to talk about the 'fuss at the Himalayan Trust' or 'that business with the watches' and proceeded to talk at length about the Trust and that business with the watches.

We also encountered at least three people who were willing to speak to us but made it clear they were planning to write their own books on Ed and would be keeping some information to themselves.

Indeed, we wondered ourselves whether another book about Ed was necessary until, having read through his writing and the other biographies, we realised that, although they all did an excellent job of recording Ed's achievements—and that is no small labour— their emphasis on what he did had not left much room for talking about what he was like. And that is the purpose of this book: to present a picture of Ed in the round.

Inevitably we will revisit his great adventures and expeditions— Everest, the South Pole, Makalu, the great Ganges journey, the time as New Zealand high commissioner to India, and the greatest of all his adventures, his aid work in Nepal through the Himalayan Trust—as the lens through which we view the man.

We will also be exploring the many paradoxes of that character: the individualist who always worked with a team; the lonely boy who ended up loved by millions; the man who could be distant from his own children but is regarded as a surrogate father by thousands of Nepali; the left-leaning thinker who accepted the highest order of chivalry from Queen Elizabeth II; the man behind the legend.

Note: We will refer to Sir Edmund Percival Hillary throughout as Ed because that is how most who knew him, including his surviving children, refer to him and because it reflects the character of the man better than Sir Ed or Sir Edmund or Hillary.

CHAPTER 1
FIRST STEPS

'My father always used to say, "Don't tell me the Hillarys are heroes. They didn't go to war."'

Alexa Johnston knew that wasn't right. But the woman addressing her went on to say that her family lived near the Hillarys in Tuakau and that among the locals this was a common view, Everest or no Everest. In fact, the Hillarys, what with father Percy's erratic behaviour and that funny religion, were regarded as a little . . . odd.

As Johnston—author of *Sir Edmund Hillary: An Extraordinary Life*—explained to the woman, Ed had served in the air force in World War II; in fact, he had gone to some lengths to do so. Ed's father, Percy, however, was a pacifist and his brother Rex had been interned as a conscientious objector.

World War I had scarred the lives of both of Ed's parents. His mother, Gertrude, had had two of her brothers killed in the conflict, and Percy had suffered head injuries at Gallipoli. Percy is thus unique in having played a part in two significant New Zealand stories, one a nation-defining disaster, the other a nation-defining triumph: Gallipoli and Everest. 'We have my grandfather's diary,'

1

says Hilary Carlisle, daughter of Ed's sister June. 'He just loved that whole adventure of going to Gallipoli, the training, being an officer. But when he was away he got shot in the nose and as part of that he became . . . no one put a label on it, but probably depressed. He had brain damage of some sort.'

Percy was invalided home in 1916. His horrendous experiences had made him a committed pacifist; in later years, he was wont to storm up the aisle of Remuera's Tudor Cinema, if a war movie was being shown, and demand that the screening cease.

Percy was a man with an iron will and a well-developed social conscience. Ed recalled how upset Percy was when he heard of food being destroyed in order to keep farmers' returns high, at a time when many people in the world were short of food. Such basic illogical injustices riled him.

He was an unusual combination of practical man and dreamer. Ed writes ruefully of his father's tendency to leave jobs unfinished—in particular the family home, which he spent many years building and which remained unfinished for much of Ed's life.

It's not hard to see in a reaction to this the seeds of the obsessive planning that was a hallmark of all Ed's endeavours.

Ed was born just after the war, on 20 July 1919. As well as his older sister June, born in 1917, there would be a younger brother, Rex, born in 1920. June later categorised the three by saying Ed had the brains, Rex had the looks and she was 'the girl'. As was customary in those times, she was expected to become a wife and mother; but there is a streak in the Hillary family character that delights in defying expectations, and June went on to teacher training and a science degree in New Zealand before moving to England, where she earned a master's degree in psychology and worked as a clinical psychologist.

Hilary describes the family dynamic thus: 'It was their mother who held the family together. She managed the money and made sure that the kids were okay. So in their teens, Mum always talks about that time when the three children and their mother formed a close group and in a way schemed against their father to get their way.'

Ed was adventurous from the start and, in childhood at least, Rex wasn't far behind. Once, the two brothers swapped bicycles— Ed on Rex's smaller bike, Rex on his brother's big one. Rex was in front and, knowing Ed would be chasing him, was going as fast as he could; but when he turned a corner, he collided with a car, bouncing off the bonnet and landing on the road. The driver was terrified he had killed Rex; Ed was merely terrified of the beating he knew Percy would give him when he saw the state of his bike.

Competition was part of the boys' relationship from the start. In an interview on the BBC's *HARDtalk* in 1999, Ed recollected his time as a beekeeper: 'I was constantly lugging around 80-pound boxes of honey. And my brother—we competed the whole time. We would rush up the hill with an 80-pound box and dump it and rush down again. And we quite enjoyed the competition. I think the sense of competition carried on over to my mountaineering.'

Although Percy was a pacifist, he was prone to fits of violent rage, and regular beatings were a feature of Ed's upbringing. Although he feared the beatings, Ed admitted he was a vexatious child with a stubborn streak to match his father's. Regardless of his guilt or innocence in any given case, Ed would never give Percy the satisfaction of admitting he had done anything wrong.

Rex's son John recounts the story of a time when Ed and Rex were told to wash their hands. 'They had to run up the stairs to the bathroom. Dad got there first and Ed grabbed him from behind to try and pull him out of the way so he could wash his hands first, but they pulled the basin out and the water was leaking everywhere.'

Simple things could be an offence in Percy's eyes. One Christmas, Rex and Ed received second-hand tennis racquets. Enraged at what he saw as their careless treatment of the gifts, Percy took the racquets and smashed them on a fence.

Ed's early years were lonely ones. He failed to make friends at primary school—which he completed two years early, thanks to some home tuition from his mother, Gertrude, who had been a teacher. This meant he was one of the smallest boys on the roll when he began secondary school—for which he was ill prepared, apart from academically. Later, when he was asked what he would change if he were to live his life over again, Ed always said there was little he would not care to repeat. But if he were given the opportunity to relive his teenage years, he said in a long interview for the US-based Academy of Achievement, he would 'dodge it like fury'.

The Hillarys' family home was in rural Tuakau, where Percy ran the local newspaper—the *Tuakau District News*—almost single-handedly, and had a sideline in beekeeping. Ed walked barefoot to primary school, rain or shine. Now he found himself spending several hours a day travelling by train from Tuakau to the intimidating halls of Auckland Grammar.

At secondary school, Ed was self-conscious. His feeling that he was a misfit who would never be accepted was exacerbated by an incident that he often recounted as a defining one in his life. In the first week, Ed turned up for gym class. As the instructor surveyed his new intake, his gaze settled on Ed and turned to a look of disdain.

'What have they sent me?' he said, loud enough for Ed to hear, and then began a detailed, humiliating catalogue of his physical deficiencies.

'Get over there with the other misfits,' said the teacher finally.

Ed was crushed. He regarded this as the beginning of his sense of 'inferiority as to how I looked', which would trouble him for a long time to come.

This was not the only unjust humiliation he suffered at the hands of a teacher. It was much later in life that he was able to bring himself to tell another such story in a magazine interview. A different teacher 'had very rigid views on what was right and what was wrong'. It was his habit to make his class stay in later than others every day, with the result that Ed could not catch the regular after-school train; he had to take a later one, which meant he got home as late as eight o'clock at night. Ed steeled himself to approach the teacher and explain this.

'Well, I can't make an exception for you,' said the teacher. 'I'll let you make your mind up what do to. You can leave on time to catch your train or I will swipe you in front of the class.'

It was exquisitely refined bullying. But it met its match in Ed's stubbornness. He said he would take the beating and leave school on time. At the end of every school day for a week Ed bent over and got thrashed with a cane in front of the class before being allowed to catch his train.

Percy and Gertrude worked out something was up and dragged the truth out of their son. Gertrude then wrote a letter for Ed to give to the school principal.

Ed and the teacher were called to the principal's office. The principal expressed his displeasure to the teacher, told him the beatings were to stop, and told Ed he was to catch his regular train from now on.

When he was asked, in his eighties, if he still hated the teacher, Ed said: 'No, I despise him.'

There was some good to be found in these experiences. Rather than let the bitterness fester into something dark, Ed developed the sensitivity to injustice that he would put to work in the world.

In later years, Ed was often asked to come back and address the students at his old school. He always delivered an inspirational message, but he did not shy away from repeating the story of his humiliations. He would warn the students about bullying; and he would admit to how frightening he had found his friendless early days at the school.

Fortunately, in the fifth and sixth form, he shot up several centimetres—he would eventually reach 188 centimetres as an adult. He enjoyed sports and learnt how to handle himself in a fight. In his memoirs, he recounted numerous violent incidents such as brawls with other boys on the train. For a boy who was used to violence at home as a way of dealing with things, fighting would have seemed a natural response.

Apart from heightening his sense of inferiority and his sensitivity to injustice, Ed was exposed to one other incident during his time at Auckland Grammar that would dominate the rest of his life. In 1935, after much persuading and haggling from his son, Percy agreed to let Ed go on a school trip to Tongariro National Park, where he saw snow for the first time; and he had his first encounter with a decent-sized mountain in the form of Mt Ruapehu, an active volcano. He was besotted.

Romanticism and a vivid imagination are traits frequently found in solitary children who spend long periods on their own, and Ed was no exception. He dreamed big. 'I was a very keen walker and, as I walked along the roads and tracks around this countryside area, I'd be dreaming. My mind would be miles away and I would be slashing villains with swords and capturing beautiful maidens and doing all sorts of heroic things.'

His fancies were fuelled by a voracious appetite for books. With his long train trips, there were periods where he was getting through a book a day. He read the books any boy of his age with an adventurous spirit would have devoured at that time—John Buchan's *The Thirty-Nine Steps*, H Rider Haggard's *King Solomon's Mines*, Edgar Rice Burroughs's *The Warlord of Mars*, and westerns—but also, incongruously, the romance and historical novels of Georgette Heyer. 'The hero was usually a rather middle-aged gentleman, a very good sword fighter, with a beautiful young lady and all the rest of it. Great sword fighting and all highly romantic, adventurous activity. I used to find these things quite entertaining. Nowadays, I find them a little on the naive side.'

He also read so many mountaineering books that 'it's rather put me off reading mountaineering books now'. He ploughed through classic volumes by Shipton and Smythe and Cherry-Garrard.

In 1935, Ed's last year at secondary school, his parents moved to the inner Auckland suburb of Remuera—not far from Auckland Grammar. He no longer needed to make the long journey between Tuakau and Auckland twice a day. Percy had parted ways with the paper, and henceforth beekeeping, which for a long time had been his hobby, now became his family's main source of income. He did not abandon journalism altogether, though—he started a beekeeping industry magazine, *New Zealand Honeybee*. Bee-keeping provided an erratic source of income, as it was dependent on the weather and the amount of honey the bees produced. But the enterprise ultimately grew to include 35 apiaries spread across 64 kilometres.

At university Ed's various interests started to coalesce. He spent two years putatively studying mathematics and science, his strongest school subjects, but with so little enthusiasm that he failed to pass a single exam. However, he did join the tramping club where, far from being consigned to the puny misfits group, he shone from the start. Tramping was something that, with his long stride and incredible stamina, he could do well.

In fact, tramping was the perfect pursuit for a solitary dreamer who had trouble making friends. As a young man, Ed was so shy that, on occasions when a pretty girl walked into a room, he would have to leave hurriedly so no one would see him blushing. Tramping gave him entry into a community that was made up of both sexes, involved in an activity that gave them a common purpose and through which they formed strong bonds.

Ed was good at team sports, but throughout his life he would focus on projects that allowed an individual to achieve his own personal goals within a group. At university, he also took classes in jujitsu and boxing, but head-to-head competition was not his style. An incident at the gym provided evidence of his capacity for reck-lessness and spontaneity, which are believed to be the hallmarks of the most successful adventurers but are actually quite rare, and mostly occur among those who meet premature deaths.

On one occasion Ed had the chance to spar with New Zealand welterweight champion Vic Calteaux. It seemed to Ed that the boxer wasn't taking his efforts seriously, so when Ed saw his chance he surprised him with a straight left to the nose. A furious Calteaux responded by beating the bejesus out of Ed; the coup de grâce a direct hit to the solar plexus. Ultimately Ed would learn the virtue of giving every action due consideration before taking it.

In 1938, Ed faced the fact that he wasn't suited to university, and defaulted to beekeeping for Percy. From then on, he would drop in and out of the business as it suited him over the years, leaving Rex to pick up the slack. He later acknowledged that he took advan-tage of Rex's good nature in doing this. Eventually the business was based in a factory at Papakura. Rex lived next to the big honey house and Ed would bunk there as he came and went, joining Rex's family for meals.

Ed would ever after be described as 'the former beekeeper'. His remarkable physiology—distinguished by extraordinary stamina, endurance and physical strength—was suited to beekeeping. It was hot, physically demanding work and in summer he would carry out his duties wearing only shorts and a hat and veil. He might get up to 300 stings in the process, he later told Alexa Johnston.

'Did they hurt?' she asked him.

'Of course they hurt,' said Ed. 'They were bee stings.'

Percy had no shortage of strong, occasionally idiosyncratic beliefs. He believed fasting would cure most sickness. As a consequence, if Ed was ever unwell, he struggled mightily never to let on to Percy so he wouldn't have to add hunger to his list of ailments.

It was about this time that the Hillary family became involved with the once-flourishing proto-New Age movement called Radiant Living, which is now remembered mainly because Ed was deeply involved in it as a young man.

English-born Herbert Sutcliffe founded the movement, which had parallels with the Christian Science teachings of Mary Baker Eddy and the transcendentalism of Ralph Waldo Emerson. It was a Christianity-based hodgepodge of dietary advice, mind over matter, physical fitness, affirmations and more. With its central tenet that good mental health was the key to good physical health, Radiant Living found a perfect adherent in Percy; and Gertrude wasn't far behind him in her enthusiasm.

The name, according to an article on NZHistory.net, referred to the belief that 'one must acknowledge the existence of the soul, "the invisible which can be visualised as a (radiant) source for good within us all ...".'. Later, when Ed had achieved his worldwide fame, Sutcliffe was to make much of the association: 'As Edmund Hillary (now Sir Edmund) is inevitably linked with the top of Mount Everest, so is Radiant Living connected with Sir Edmund,' he wrote. Ed travelled with Sutcliffe as his assistant in 1940. World War II would eventually sever Ed's involvement with Radiant Living—he was not inclined to return to it when the war was over, although he continued to be something of a spiritual quester. Over the next few years, he looked into many esoteric religions, but his practical nature meant none could win his allegiance. His studies did, however, leave him with a tolerance of a wide variety of beliefs.

When World War II broke out and it looked likely his sons would be conscripted, Percy took advantage of a provision that allowed exemption for reserved occupations, including beekeeping. He got his elder son Ed off the hook first. But he did it without telling Ed—who was not pleased.

Percy then learnt to his dismay that only one exemption per family was allowed. Rex would have to go to war.

Ironically—and devastatingly—Rex, unlike Ed, was a conscientious objector on philosophical grounds. The older boy would have been happy to sign up; Rex was not and, following his conscience, he spent four years of the war in a detention camp. 'And Ed changed his mind of course and decided to go to war, and I think if he'd only made his mind up in the first place, my life could have been quite different,' Rex told Ed's friend and chronicler Tom Scott years later—with some understatement.

How Ed felt about what happened to Rex may be assumed from the fact that he does not refer to it in either of his autobiographies. Ed could, of course, simply have gone to war from the very start, but Percy's will was so strong that he was initially unable to withstand it. Eventually, Percy gave in and Ed finally joined the Royal New Zealand Air Force in 1944.

He wanted to be a pilot, but the authorities didn't see him as pilot material and he trained as a navigator. While training in the South Island, Ed encountered more mountains and did a few solo climbs, none too ambitious. From the camp, however, he could see 2884-metre, snowy-topped Mt Tapuaenuku, and he became determined to make an ascent. He arranged a three-day leave.

A potential climbing partner pulled out at the last minute so Ed decided to go it alone. A friend took him part of the way on his motorbike and Ed then walked 8 kilometres to a farm, where he stayed overnight, and another 24 kilometres the next day. He overnighted again before commencing his climb—having ignored advice from the few souls he encountered to abandon his solo plan. He reached the top and returned safely. The next day he walked another 32 kilometres before getting a lift.

He was exultant. He had climbed his first proper mountain. Nothing could compare with this.

He was also involved in physical activity at ground level. A competent rugby player, he played in a championship team for his squadron. His ability had been noted by a member of a team from another camp, whose side was preparing for a championship final. There wasn't much between the rival teams, but his team was down two players due to illness. Would Ed and a friend be willing to jump the fence and fill in?

Ed threw himself into the game in such a robustly physical fashion that afterwards one of the spectators, a supporter of the losing side, was keen to settle the score off the field. On reflection, Ed acknowledged that his conduct on the field had been too aggressive, and he liked himself the less for it.

Ed enjoyed his war service. He qualified as a navigator and spent time stationed in the Pacific Islands, serving on Catalina flying boats. His already well-developed social conscience was pricked when he met a poor Fijian boy, who begged him first for a piece of bread and then for money. It was a vignette that stayed with him.

In a navigation exercise, he took a plane off course. This unchar-acteristic error occurred because he had taken the word of his pilot, who had misidentified a piece of land as a reference point, rather than trusting his own navigational skills. He would generally follow his own counsel from then on—no matter who was nominally in charge.

Ed never came near armed combat, though he did contract malaria. In one memorable incident, he and his friend Ron Ward shot a crocodile, memorialised by a photo in which Ed's grin is nearly as wide as that of the deceased beast. Despite numerous subsequent attempts, the pair failed to claim a second croc.

Ed's war came to an end in near disaster. En route from Tulagi in the Solomon Islands to Halavo Bay, Florida Island, he and Ward were about to take off in their flying boat when a bump dislodged a full petrol tank inside their plane, and it fell and burst into flames. Before Ed, who was not wearing a shirt, could jump clear of his blazing craft, a wave knocked him off his feet and he fell onto the flames. He then managed to roll off and into the sea.

Ed suffered second-degree burns; the pain was exacerbated by having to swim 450 metres in salt water and then walk 800 metres under the blazing sun before reaching help.

He was taken to hospital first at Tulagi, then to Guadalcanal, and shot full of morphine and antibiotics. He was told to expect to spend months in hospital before achieving anything like a full recovery. By his second week he was able to walk around for short periods. By the third week he was bored and restless. He badgered and cajoled until, still bandaged, he was allowed out of hospital, though not off the islands. Finally it was acknowledged that he could recover as well in Auckland as in the Solomons and he was discharged from the air force and sent home.

Ed's recuperative abilities were extraordinary and played a large part in his later achievements. For now, however, it wasn't clear what these achievements might involve. He intended to spend his time beekeeping and mountain climbing. But when he learnt, to his surprise, that Percy didn't actually have a place for him in the business when he left the air force, he headed to the South Island and started looking around for new challenges.

CHAPTER TWO
ON TOP

George Mallory famously wanted to climb Everest because it was there. Ed Hillary's actions suggest he wanted to climb it because he wanted to be there first.

Unlike many young people in years to come, Ed did not grow up dreaming that one day he would climb the world's highest mountain. He hadn't even seen a mountain until he was sixteen. But from the time he climbed his first 'decent mountain' it was his passion.

In the post-war years Ed climbed as often as he could. In 1945 he became an associate member of the New Zealand Alpine Club (NZAC) and that year scaled Kitchener, Sealy, De la Beche, Hamilton and Malte Brun. In January of the next year he ascended Mt Cook with his mentor, the great mountaineer Harry Ayres, who would teach Ed much of the climber's craft. Some of Ed's earliest efforts at writing were accounts of his climbs that he penned for the NZAC's *New Zealand Alpine Journal*.

As a member of a party that included Ayres and Christchurch climber Ruth Adams, he made the first ascent of the south ridge of Mt Cook on 6 February 1948.

Three days later, there was a character-testing incident when Adams fell and injured herself in an attempt on La Perouse. While the others went for help, Ed stayed with Adams for what turned into a night spent at the scene, relying on supplies that were air-dropped in. 'Had a party set itself the task of finding the most inaccessible spot in the high central alps in which to become involved in an accident, it could hardly have done better than the main divide between Mt Hicks and La Perouse,' wrote MJP Glasgow in the *New Zealand Alpine Journal*.

Adams needed to be stretchered out. It was not possible to return the way they had come, so she was effectively carried over the top of the mountain and down the other side. The rescue party took 48 hours just to reach Adams and Ed. Several other climbers—who would later figure in the history of the first ascent of Mt Everest— were also involved: Norm Hardie, Earle Riddiford and Bill Beaven. It remains one of the most dramatic and difficult rescues in New Zealand's long alpine history.

Ed liked being first, and he would be the first to climb many New Zealand peaks in the following few years. When his sister June got married in England in 1949, their parents, financially buoyed by an excellent honey season, travelled to the wedding. They stayed on, and early the next year there came a somewhat imperious instruction to Ed to get himself over there as they required someone to drive them around Europe. He did so—and took every opportunity to practise his climbing skills on some European peaks, including the Eiger. At one point he climbed five mountains in five days.

While Ed was in Europe, he received a letter from George Lowe with a most intriguing suggestion.

A Hastings-born school teacher and mountaineer, Lowe was a man of great warmth and wit—and he was almost Ed's peer as a climber. They had met on a bus at Mt Cook and quickly developed a firm bond. Lowe would remain a lifelong friend and colleague of Ed's. Both men had had self-doubts to overcome. George's equivalent of Ed's earlier scrawny physique was an arm that had been broken and set badly. This had prevented him from serving during the war, but it would not prevent him from doing much else.

George had written to tell Ed that the first-ever New Zealand Himalayan climbing party was being formed. Would Ed like to be involved? He certainly would.

The other two climbers in the party were Earle Riddiford, a lawyer, and the athletic and entertaining Ed Cotter. Back home the four got to know each other, honing their skills in the South Island, where they prepared for the expedition by making the first ascent of Mt Elie De Beaumont from the Maximilian Ridge. It is a difficult mountain to access and is most commonly climbed from the Mt Cook side of the Tasman Glacier.

The purpose of their intended Everest expedition was twofold, as Ed wrote in the *Alpine Journal*: to see if a practicable route existed up the mountain from the southern, or Nepalese, side; and to find out if the post-monsoon snow conditions were suitable for a major attack on the peak. These were crucial preparatory steps. An actual assault would only come later.

In mountaineering circles there was no greater challenge than a successful ascent of Mt Everest. The world's highest peak takes its English name from a British surveyor-general of India who never laid eyes on it. In Tibetan it is called more poetically Chomolungma (mother goddess of the universe) and in Nepali Sagarmatha (goddess of the sky). It is 8848 metres high, and natural forces squeeze it up a few millimetres every year.

Before Ed, the name most associated with Everest was that of George Mallory—that most romantic of mountaineers. Mallory was a member of the first British Everest reconnaissance expedition in 1921 and several subsequent expeditions before the 1924 British Mount Everest Expedition, during which he perished on the mountain. Many other people had died trying to scale the peak, including seven Sherpas in 1922 alone and an eccentric English soldier and mystic, Maurice Wilson, who attempted a solo climb in 1934. For the misfit, scrawny, shy kid from the 'odd' family, being the first person to climb the world's highest mountain would redeem it all.

A turning point in the history of attempts on Everest came in 1950 when the Nepalese Government agreed to allow parties to attempt the mountain from Nepal, on the southern side. Previous missions had attacked from Tibet, on the northern side of the mountain. The Nepalese Government decided to allow a different country every year to have a go.

The members of the New Zealand expedition gained valuable experience of climbing conditions in the area when Riddiford and Cotter made the first ascent of 7242-metre Mukut Parbat. Riddiford had been fighting illness, and Ed reported later, in *Nothing Venture, Nothing Win*, that the lawyer's success on this occasion taught him a valuable lesson about just how willpower could be deployed to overcome physical obstacles. Ed himself developed formidable strength of will, but in years to come he would find out that even the strongest willpower was not enough for some challenges.

Ed's social conscience was also reawakened by the gap he observed between the poverty that was so prevalent in this part of the world and the high standard of living back home in New Zealand.

The party was headed to New Zealand when they received a telegram that could fairly be described as a letter bomb, so great was its divisive effect on them. The missive was from the esteemed Everest pioneer Eric Shipton, who had made his first assault on the mountain in 1938. It contained an invitation to join another British reconnaissance expedition.

According to Ed, he had written to Shipton when he had heard that the Englishman was planning such a mission—effectively inviting Shipton to invite the New Zealanders. At the same time, NZAC had written to their northern counterparts suggesting there were some well-qualified climbers in the club who could be an asset to the British expedition.

It was the opportunity of a lifetime. The only problem was that the invitation stipulated that the climbers would have to provide their own supplies; and it was for only two people. But which two?

Ed Hillary, obviously, as far as Ed was concerned. He knew he should get back to the bees, but the chance to get to Everest outweighed any scruples about leaving Rex to mind the store yet again. And he could afford it, because he still had the remnants of a nest egg acquired during six weeks' work on a South Island hydroelectric project.

George Lowe and Earle Riddiford obviously felt the same way. The dispute that developed was too much for the genial Cotter, who withdrew any claim for inclusion. And it has to be said that someone who could walk away from that fight probably wouldn't have made it to the top of Everest.

It appears that Lowe and Riddiford acknowledged Ed should go, as he was the superior climber. On skills alone, Lowe would seem to have had the next best claim, but he was broke whereas Riddiford was still flush. Riddiford also told Lowe he didn't have the necessary drive. Lowe was livid, but he also lost the argument.

Ed described being haunted by the sight of Lowe's disappointed face as the party split up. For himself, he had lost the chance to fulfill a dream with his best friend; he would instead be travelling with a fellow climber he admitted he disliked.

Ed sent a telegram to Percy telling him the bees would have to get on without him. Although Ed was now in his thirties, he still felt dominated by his father, and the letter included a plea to 'forgive your erring son'. Not that there was any way Ed would change his mind.

Ed would now have to prove to Percy that he was doing something worthwhile—a tall order when, for Ed's generation, to be in your thirties and have neither a job nor wife and children was out of the ordinary. According to Tom Scott, Ed at this stage felt like a borderline failure, which of course only fuelled his desire to prove himself.

Shipton was an explorer to the core—he would never take the same route twice to a destination if he could try an alternative. On this trip, while some of the party were left to explore the forbidding Khumbu Icefall—the first obstacle to an ascent—he and Ed went climbing together and chanced upon the Western Cwm, a hidden valley that appeared to provide a previously undiscovered southern route to Everest. This was yet another turning point in the history of attempts on the mountain and would remain—along with his success in talent-spotting Ed and, eventually, George Lowe—Shipton's greatest contribution to the ultimately successful effort.

The party split up and planned to return to the area the following year. But this time, Ed made sure George Lowe was included. The 1952 group would not, however, be attempting the world's highest peak. Hanging heavily over them was the knowledge that the Swiss had the right to attempt Everest this year. Britain's turn would come a year later. Ed had a twinge of resentment when he first heard this—he was already experiencing proprietorial feelings about the mountain.

Once he was back home, he saw to the paperwork and filed an expense claim with the Alpine Club in London; he even claimed reimbursement for money spent on cups of tea. In reply, the club gently explained to its colonial offspring that 'gentlemen are expected to pay for their own cups of tea'. Ed was quick to point out that, being New Zealanders, he and Earle could not possibly be gentlemen—and the club eventually gave way on the point.

The main focus of the Shipton group's efforts in 1952 was an attempt—ultimately unsuccessful—on 8201-metre Cho Oyu. Ed, of course, did not stop at one mountain. He and George Lowe roamed the region, successfully climbing eight peaks, attempting the Changtse and exploring the Barun peaks, with the occasional day off in between. They concluded their peregrinations in the village of Sedua before floating down the wild Arun River on airbeds. George Lowe reported, in a piece he wrote for the NZAC *Alpine Journal*, that Ed punctuated the hair-raising journey by tossing off quips such as 'How long can we last on a chocolate bar?' and 'Obviously we can't go on like this forever.'

The expedition also provided much valuable experience of living and climbing in high altitude and extreme conditions—knowledge that would be invaluable when it came time to take on Chomolungma itself. They were as well prepared as it was possible to be, and all the signs were favourable for a Shipton-led attempt to climb Mt Everest in 1953. Until Shipton was fired.

His replacement was John Hunt.

Britain was desperate for this mission to be a success and had already made numerous errors in earlier attempts. Leadership had been one of the problems. 'They had put a lot of bad people in charge,' says Pat Booth, the Auckland journalist who would cover Ed's career over several decades. 'An Australian climber by the name of George Finch [father of actor Peter] had got to 8320 metres in 1922 with Mallory. He was an expert on oxygen but he and Mallory didn't get on and for various reasons he didn't go again.'

Hunt was a veteran of three previous Himalayan expeditions. He had won the Sandhurst Sword of Honour, commanded an Indian brigade in World War II and been awarded the DSO in Italy. He had trained troops in snow and mountain warfare, so was used to leading men in Himalayan-type conditions.

'The Poms had just won a war, but lost the peace,' says Tom Scott, explaining the mindset. In 1953, Great Britain placed much hope in the new Queen, who would be crowned that year. 'England was still a bombsite with rationing and queues for this and that. It owed America a fortune. At the start of a new age with a beautiful young Queen they wanted to celebrate the coronation with a gift that would be the last terrestrial prize.'

Firing Shipton had been a tough decision for the organisers, and was a terrible personal blow not just for Shipton but for Ed, who was distraught at the news. But history shows the choice was correct, even if it was hard to see at the time. It also taught Ed a valuable lesson—that affection and sentiment were not sufficient qualities to earn someone a place in a team. When it came to choosing the right man for a job, it was talent and ability alone that would decide the matter. Feelings didn't come into it.

Despite two concerted efforts, the Swiss did not reach the summit of Everest during their year. But they came close. Included in their team was a most experienced Everest hand—the Sherpa sirdar (head man) Tenzing Norgay, who had already been involved in four attempts on the mountain. He and Swiss climber Raymond Lambert had been forced to turn back just 300 metres from the summit the previous year.

According to Scott, Ed and Lowe had thought it unsporting of the Swiss to have two tries—one in the spring and one in the autumn. 'They were sick with worry the Swiss would get there. Ed desperately wanted that mountain. He was the best climber in the world. George was the second best. So when the Swiss failed Ed was delighted. Next it was the English turn. In 1954 it would be France's turn. They had only one climbing season in which to do it.'

Looking back at the failed Swiss attempt, Ed used the special tone of patronising graciousness that he reserved for people who tried and failed to do something that he achieved. 'We wished the Swiss no harm at all and they'd really put in a very good assault on the mountain,' he told Tom Scott in his documentary *Hillary: A View from the Top.*

The story of Everest is populated by many 'nearly men'— climbers who almost got there but, for one reason or other, did not. Some—such as the gifted New Zealand climber Norm Hardie, one of the few men in the world besides Ed, Tenzing and Lowe who probably could have made it to the top—did not even get to Nepal. Others, such as George Lowe, were selected for the party but not for the attempt. Harry Ayres missed out for political reasons. He was on the long list and Ed desperately wanted him to come, but Hunt decided to limit the number of New Zealanders to two. And then there were Charles Evans and Tom Bourdillon, who came within two hours of the top but turned back because they would not have managed the descent if they had continued.

Norm Hardie still feels the disappointment of not being included in Hunt's team. There is no questioning his ability. He was in the group of four who were first to climb Kangchenjunga, the world's third highest mountain, believed by some to be a more difficult ascent than Everest. Unfortunately, as Hardie says, 'People still don't know where Kangchenjunga is. They mix it up with Kilimanjaro . . . even very few in Nepal know about Kangchenjunga.' According to journalist Desmond Doig, when Hardie reached the top of Kangchenjunga 'in respect of local sentiment he left the last few tantalizing feet unscaled'.

Hardie might have expected to get the opportunity to join the team. He was a good friend of the expedition's deputy leader, Charles Evans. 'When the Everest thing came up Evans pressed Hunt to include me,' says Hardie. Hunt interviewed Hardie, who made a good impression. But the expedition leader was frank and told the climber that Evans was the only one pressing his claim. He pointed out that Hardie had no Himalayan experience; and he told him he had already accepted Ed and Lowe as members of his expedition. At the time there was no shortage of English climbers from well-established clubs fighting to be included and Hunt was under pressure not to include any New Zealanders at all, let alone three.

This background of national selection helps explain why Hunt chose who he did to make the eventual final assaults on the peak. His first choice was the more politically palatable pairing of his British deputy, Charles Evans, and his British oxygen expert, Tom Bourdillon. His second choice was a Sherpa and a New Zealander, who had shown themselves to be the toughest climbers in the group.

By 13 April base camp had been set up below the Khumbu Icefall. They had six weeks within which to achieve their goal.

The impression of Ed at this time of his life as an energetic mountain goat bounding around the Himalayas from rock to rock is reinforced in a tribute party member George Band wrote at the time of Ed's death: 'Ed would be among the first to enjoy a quick dip before breakfast in one of the icy streams flowing down from the glaciers to the north. Then to warm up, he might borrow Mike Westmacott's butterfly net to try to chase and capture an elusive blue morpho.'

Ed had natural gifts that made him the right man to reach the top of Everest first. He was extraordinarily strong—an everyday strength, not from working out in a gym but borne of day after long day of hard work from an early age. 'He could lift honey boxes on and off trucks at the age of ten, and they are really heavy,' says Tom Scott. 'He had a raw-boned farmer's strength. That sort of work builds stamina as well. George Lowe was incredibly fit, and he said when tramping no one could compete with Ed or keep up with his phenomenal pace.'

He had also got used to working at high altitude where, at 8000 metres, for example, the oxygen is 75 per cent less than at sea level. 'I was hoping for the documentary to film his fountain pen diary,' says Scott. 'I thought, this will be great, we'll film pages of his diary at base camp and then later film his handwriting deteriorating [as he got higher]. Here is proof of what altitude does. And he gave me his diary and it was as literate and copperplate at 27,500 feet as lower down. That's how fit he was.'

Ed was fully conscious of his own physical and psychological advantages on the trip. 'I knew I could go up the mountainside faster than anybody else,' he told the *New Zealand Listener* in 2007, 'and this also gave me a great deal of confidence—probably why I got to the top of Everest . . . I knew that I could move fast, even at high altitude, and faster than anyone else in the team who were good climbers. I was also somewhat competitive, I have to admit. I was quite prepared to compete with companions on the trip. We were off on a climb up a ridge to get a good look at the possible routes on the mountain and then we would rush down again and I always made sure that I got up higher first and that I got down first. There was simply no doubt in my mind that that's what I was going to do and I did it. So you know that gave me a great deal of confidence when I knew that even these renowned climbers—that I could leave them for dead if I had to.'

When Ed was roped to Wilfrid Noyce, who was in charge of boots on the expedition, and Noyce was following faster than Ed liked, Ed sped up until the rope was taut, and he made sure it stayed taut.

The expedition used aluminium ladders to get across the many crevasses they had to negotiate. It was a hair-raising means of transport that involved placing the ladder across the gap then gingerly crawling over rung by rung. Ed insisted on being first across.

Other members might have been fitter, or more ambitious, or had more experience. Some were definitely better technical climbers. But Ed had the right combination of qualities to get to the top.

'He resented being classified as a simple uncomplicated climber who happened to be in the right place at the right time,' says Scott. 'There was more to it than that. No Ed Hillary, no Everest. There are defining moments on that mountain where if Ed hadn't been there it would not have been climbed. He was resented for it, but he was just so much better than the others. It's hard to handle when someone is that conspicuously better. The Poms thought it was their mountain, but there was one Pom who . . . knew he could get to the top and gave him uncritical approval—Eric Shipton. He knew Ed had greatness in him.'

Initially Ed and George Lowe did much together, but Ed was planning from the start to maximise his chances of getting to the top and knew Hunt would be unlikely to send two New Zealanders under any circumstances.

'When it became clear to me I wouldn't be allowed to climb with George Lowe,' says Ed in *A View from the Top*, 'I looked around for someone of equal fitness and strong motivation. The most likely person seemed to be Tenzing.'

If there was a moment when Ed and Tenzing became a team,

it was when they were moving roped together and Ed, instead of crossing a crevasse on the nearby ice bridge, decided to jump across. As he did the edge of the ice snapped and he fell. Tenzing jammed his axe into the snow, the rope between the two went tight and Ed gradually returned to the surface. As John Hunt wrote: 'That no harm came of it was due to the foresight and skill of Tenzing.'

Fellow climber Graeme Dingle says Ed and Tenzing had one unlikely characteristic in common that played a part in their success. 'Curiously both Tenzing and Ed carried a similar kind of chip. In spite of the drive that the British should be the first at the top, the irony is they didn't get there. The two foreigners got there first and they both positioned themselves to do that. They both had sufficient inferiority complexes to achieve it and the physical ability to do it.'

Ed did much to draw Hunt's attention to his fitness and other exemplary qualities. He and Tenzing persuaded Hunt to let them do a fast climb from base camp to advance base and back to test the open-circuit oxygen equipment. This was a demonstration of ability and stamina that was clearly designed to show their suitability for a summit attempt. According to Alexa Johnston, 'they had climbed 1,200 metres in just over four hours, instead of the usual nine hours spread over three days'. Hunt noticed.

At another point, a group of Sherpas staged a kind of mutiny and refused to go on to complete an essential stage of the mission. Ed asked Hunt to let him and Tenzing go up—a four-and-a-half-hour trek—and spur them on. Hunt agreed. Tenzing exhorted his men to carry on and he and Ed accompanied them to their goal before returning. This was a major turning point in the expedition, and one that no other members would have had the physical ability or moral authority to bring about.

Hunt had decided there would be two attempts on the summit. The first would be by Evans and Bourdillon using closed-circuit oxygen equipment. If that failed Tenzing and Hillary would be sent up with the open-circuit gear. The former system involved recirculating oxygen carried by the climbers; the latter used oxygen taken from the atmosphere.

There was never any doubt Ed deserved his place—he was, simply, the best. Still, emotions ran high when the choice was made. Mike Ward, team doctor and superlative climber, was furious when he found out that he had been placed in the reserves, and lashed out at Hunt. George Band later described the New Zealanders as pushy. It's an accusation seldom made against New Zealanders, but Ed and George Lowe would have been the last to disagree with the assessment.

Before the final attempts there had been a lot of English courtesy on display: 'After you.' 'No, no, after you.' But mountaineering isn't an activity that has a lot of room for such niceties. And Ed certainly had no room for it—he always sought to be out in front. While the others were debating precedence he would charge through the middle, yelling 'Gangway!' at the top of his voice.

On their return from dealing with the Sherpa mutiny, Tenzing and Ed encountered Evans and Bourdillon beginning the first attempt to get to the top. Their attempt ended in failure, defeated by—among other factors—a diminishing supply of oxygen. It is possible that if they had used the open-circuit system they would have had sufficient reserves to get there and back.

It is an indication of how Ed's candour developed over the years that, whereas in *Nothing Venture, Nothing Win* he says he was pleased when the first party set off for the summit, in *View from the Summit* he says he was pleased when they returned without reaching it.

Ed's courage and impulsiveness were always balanced with intelligence and planning. On the climb, he obsessively calculated and recalculated how much oxygen he and Tenzing had, could get away with, and needed. It was a great moment when he chanced upon two bottles that Evans and Bourdillon had abandoned, just as his stock was running low. He also felt sure that Tenzing and Lambert had failed to reach the top, a year to the day earlier, because they had not been sufficiently hydrated, having relied on cheese and snow melted over a candle for sustenance. Ed was in charge of melting snow on Primus stoves to provide water, and made sure everyone kept their fluids up.

Ed told the story hundreds of times of how he and Tenzing Norgay became the first people to stand on the top of Mt Everest. He described the later stages to the BBC in 1999:

'The oxygen equipment was not all that sophisticated. It only had a pressure gauge on it, so I never really knew just how much oxygen remained. I had to work out from the pressure how much oxygen remained. All the way up my brain was working fairly energetically . . . I don't remember feeling any particular fear until about halfway along, where there was this rock step which is now called the Hillary Step.'

This was the crucial moment, the very last obstacle between the climber and the summit. 'The Hillary Step was one of the harder bits of the climb of the mountain and I decided that I would pioneer it, as it were,' he told the *Listener*. 'It had a rock face on one side and a big ice face on the other and I decided that I could scramble up between the rock face and the ice face. So that's what I did and I got up and got to the top and then I yelled out to Tenzing to come on up and he duly came up and then I carried on cutting steps. I cut steps almost from the top to the bottom of the mountain and I cut steps along the final narrow ridge along the top with Tenzing not too far behind.'

And with that, at 11.30 am on 29 May 1953, placing first one size 12 boot and then the other where no one had ever set foot before, Ed Hillary, closely followed by Tenzing Norgay, achieved what so many others had only dreamed of doing.

His overriding emotion, he always said, was a feeling of relief. He and Tenzing looked at each other. The reserved New Zealander took Tenzing's hand to give it a hearty shake. The Sherpa, nearly 20 centimetres shorter than his lanky companion, threw his arms around the climber in a joyful embrace.

There was work to be done. Ed photographed Tenzing triumphant, holding aloft his ice axe and the flags they had taken with them and which they would leave there—the ensigns of India, Great Britain, Nepal and the United Nations, but not that of New Zealand. Nor, in a move that would mystify many over the years, did he get Tenzing to take a photo of him. His explanation was always that he didn't think Tenzing had ever used a camera before and now wasn't the time to learn.

He turned 360 degrees and took photos at every point, capturing every ridge below so that there could be no doubt that he was shooting from the very top.

He looked around for any sign that Mallory might have been there but could find none. And he gazed across at forbidding Makalu—another apparently impregnable peak—and saw what he thought might be a route to its top. When a French party became the first to summit Makalu, it was this route they followed.

Ed and Tenzing were both carrying a few talismans to be left on the mountain, and these they now placed in the snow. Lollies and a coloured pencil that Tenzing's daughter had given him; and a cross that John Hunt had asked Ed to carry.

It was time to descend to base camp—to a place in history and a state of celebrity Ed could not have begun to imagine. He took a few stones from the highest point in the world as souvenirs; and finally—his effort to keep his fluids up having been as successful as everything else on this day—he paused to relieve himself on Chomolungma.

CHAPTER 3
DOWN TO EARTH

Others have climbed Everest more than once. Ed's son Peter has been there twice; once on a day when 78 people reached the summit. Apa Sherpa has made a record 21 ascents. A Sherpa couple has been married on the summit. But Ed didn't ever consider repeating that particular climb. For him, once something was done, it was done.

'Neither Tenzing nor I ever had the feeling,' he said. 'We were first and as a consequence never had the motivation to go up again. Nowadays everyone wants to go up more than once—but they didn't have the pleasure of going up first.'

In fact, he never pulled off another mountaineering coup, despite several attempts. His other major achievements were in many different areas. He did, however, have other climbing ambitions involving Everest. According to Tom Scott, Ed had expressed the ambition to attempt a solo ascent; one from the north; and one without oxygen. All these feats were eventually achieved, though not by Ed. However, few people outside the mountaineering community remember who achieved these other firsts.

It was 1 pm when George Lowe, from his position at Camp VIII, sighted Ed and Tenzing briefly on the south summit. At 2 pm he saw them again. Moving quickly he set out to meet them and hear the good news, in Ed's masterpiece of insouciance: 'Well, George, we knocked the bastard off.'

The group camped for the night before making their final descent back to join the main group. The other team members were in various states of suspense, but none more so than John Hunt, who tried to decipher the party's demeanour as they approached. When Lowe gestured with his ice axe towards Everest towering behind and gave a thumbs-up, Hunt knew his expedition had been victorious.

As they grew closer an emotional Hunt ran forward and embraced his assault party in a scene that combined relief, triumph and exhaustion. For some of the others in the party, there would have been a niggling realisation that no one else would have the chance to be the first man on Everest: that honour had gone to a New Zealander. Although for posterity, the media and absolutely anyone who asked, everyone agreed it was a team effort, few people remember the name of the team or its members, apart from Ed and Tenzing.

Not long before Hunt died, Tom Scott interviewed him in England.

'You in your heart of hearts must have wanted two Englishmen there,' Scott said.

'How could I have wanted it any other way?' admitted Hunt.

'Would you say that on camera?'

'Heavens, no.'

'Well, we'll roll the camera and see if you change your mind. Sir John, did you want two Englishmen on the top first?'

'I was thrilled that it was Ed and Tenzing who were the first to stand on top,' said Hunt.

And then he winked at Scott.

Ed's emotions had been held at bay until he was back with the rest of the group. 'We all got to our high camp and sort of celebrated and then we carried on down to base camp, and down at base camp we had a really good celebration. One of the other members of the party . . . had a bottle of rum and I wasn't really a drinker at all in those days, but we all had a sip of rum. Now—this is at an altitude of oh, close on 20,000 feet—when you drink alcohol at that sort of altitude, it has quite a strong effect, so we all got a little bit tiddly.'

Other reactions would follow swiftly, much to Ed's surprise. He seems to have genuinely believed that very few people outside the mountaineering community would be much interested in what he had done. Mountain climbing, after all, was not an activity with a huge public following.

The Times of London was an expedition sponsor, with rights to John Hunt's own account of the expedition. But it did not even try to keep the initial announcement—which it received first and which came on the morning of Elizabeth II's coronation day—to itself. Every newspaper in the world seemed captivated by the story of the ascent, with its added patina of royal glamour. Ed expected that, once any small fuss there might be had died down, he would be left to get on with his life. He might get the occasional speaking request and invitation to contribute to the NZAC *Alpine Journal*. And there were always the bees, although he had done a good job of finding reasons not to go back to them for some time now.

Percy certainly expected him to go back to the bees—and the sooner the better. He soon realised that Ed's achievement was seen as quite something, but he never indicated that he thought there was much point to the exercise, although he and Gertrude did send Hunt a congratulatory telegram. Gertrude's response was more enthusiastic than Percy's. John Hillary remembers being 'on my grandmother's lounge room floor with my mother and we were cutting up newspaper clippings from the *Herald* and putting them in a scrapbook'.

As for Norm Hardie—and probably many other climbers who had harboured an ambition to be first atop Everest—he says his feelings when he heard the news were 'mixed'. The conqueror of Kangchenjunga has a tart summary of why the Everest climb drew such acclaim: 'It's the highest in the world. Two, a pronounceable name. Three, James Morris and Hunt were very good PR men. Evans on Kangchenjunga was totally shy and self-restrained—a great leader, but not a public man. Four, as sponsor, *The Times* was a very reputable paper so all the sources paid for the story. Many previous attempts on Everest with Mallory and other thrillers had kept up British interest in Everest.'

Back home the news was announced by acting Prime Minister Keith Holyoake who, overcome with coronation fever, placed the achievement firmly in an imperial context: 'I am able to announce that a newsflash has just come through advising us that the New Zealander, Hillary, has succeeded in conquering Mount Everest . . . If the news is correct, and I'm assured absolutely that it is, then our New Zealander Hillary has climbed to the top of the world. He has put the British race and New Zealand on the top of the world. And what a magnificent coronation present for the Queen. How proud we all are that this is from our loyal little New Zealand.'

Holyoake would be less enthusiastic about Ed in years to come.

The new Queen responded instantly by knighting Ed—to his chagrin. Customarily those being offered that honour are asked if they are willing to accept. Ed being incommunicado, the New Zealand prime minister took the liberty of accepting on his behalf and Ed got the news in the mail, handed over by a highly amused George Lowe.

For a high achiever it would have been a disconcerting early sign that he might not always be in total control of where his life was going. 'I wasn't all that happy about the knighthood to be totally honest,' Ed recalled in his *HARDtalk* interview. 'I was just a rough old country boy. A beekeeper. I couldn't see me wandering around the farm with a knighthood doing the same simple things I'd been doing for years.'

His attitude to honours may have changed over the years, as he never expressed any reluctance when, in 1995, he was elevated to the highest order of chivalry and made a Knight of the Garter—an honour that John Hunt had received in 1979.

Tenzing received the George Medal, the civilian equivalent of the Victoria Cross. This too Ed cavilled about: 'I felt it would have been more appropriate if he also had received a title. Everybody involved in these things in Britain said he can't get a title because inhabitants of India or Nepal are not permitted to have a British title. I think that's rubbish. I think if he had received a title everyone in India and Nepal would have been thrilled to bits.'

He didn't have to wait long to be asked a question he would be asked over and over again for the rest of his life: Who really got to the top first? This was by turns annoying, amusing, tedious, rude and ridiculous.

We can be certain Ed made it to the top for two reasons. One is that he wanted to be first. In all his writing and speaking about Everest, he made no secret of his ambition to be part of the project and then, once on the mountain, to be part of the summiting team. It's hard to imagine that, as he and Tenzing set out, he would suddenly have lost all interest in the question of precedence; that he wouldn't have made sure that it would be his boot that first planted itself on the peak. All his friends and fellow team members describe Ed ploughing ahead in any situation, whether crawling across a crevasse on a ladder or bounding towards the next campsite. He did not do second.

The other reason we know for sure Ed was first without his telling us is that his deeply ingrained honesty would not have allowed a lie—or even a misconception—to gain currency. If Tenzing really had been first, Ed would have been the first to say so.

In the early days Ed and Tenzing had been happy to say that Ed was first, Tenzing next. However, as the days went by and the team made their way homewards through Nepal and the crowds grew ever bigger, so too did their enthusiasm for the notion that the local had summited first. Eventually, Ed and Tenzing went with the flow. It has been suggested that, as well as going with the flow, Tenzing may have actively muddied the waters.

In later years the official line became that they got there together; and Hunt credited the whole team with the ascent. Of course it was a team effort—a solo ascent wouldn't be made until 1980.

The team could not have done it without Ed, but Ed couldn't have done it without the team.

Ed hummed and hah-ed somewhat over what to say on the issue over the years. Perhaps the best attempt at diplomacy was this account to the *Listener*'s Maggie Barry: 'That was the way it was. I mean, I had unquestionably set foot on the little cone of the summit and Tenzing had followed very effectively behind . . . in actual fact, to say that we reached the summit almost together was as good a description as you would really require.'

That was the official line back home. His son Peter recalls: 'It was always, always in our household: "We did it together. Tenzing and I were a team, we climbed the summit first," and that's just the way it was.

'The reality was in Tenzing's biography he did say that Ed had stepped on first and [Tenzing] came up behind him, and Dad continued to say, "We climbed it together, we climbed it together" and it was only in the most recent autobiography that he did say that he went up there first. The only reason he did that, he told me, was because Tenzing said it himself—so, he thought, I will too.'

Ed told a slightly different version to the *Listener*: 'When Tenzing died, I decided . . . well, I mean, if someone asked me who got to the top first, oh, Tenzing's dead, he's done a great job—I see no reason why I shouldn't mention that I actually set foot on top first. But only if people asked. I felt a bit poorly about it first and of course Tenzing's grandson resented this bitterly. But I felt that for ten or fifteen years I had held my peace and that it would be fair for me to actually tell what had happened. After all, he reached the top too.'

But back in 1953, Ed had not been happy as the Tenzing mania along the route back from Everest grew ever more frenzied. He found himself the subject of a cartoon for the first time—there would be many more over the years. The image was on a placard that was hoisted over the crowd. It showed a triumphant Tenzing alone on top of Everest. Some metres below, attached to the Sherpa by a rope, lay Ed on his back, relaxing while Tenzing did all the work.

Ed thought this was funny at first, but not for long. And when an enthusiastic member of the crowd leapt onto the car carrying him and bellowed, 'Long live Tenzing' in Ed's ear, his temper got the better of him and he shoved the young man to the ground.

By now Ed should have begun to realise that this was the start of something big. 'I had no idea that the media and the public in general would be as interested as they turned out to be. I think I was a rather naive sort of person in those days.'

In fact, this was Ed's first day at his new job for life—Conqueror of Everest. It was not a position anyone had had before, and for the next 55 years he would effectively make it up day by day as he went along. And he would make the most of it.

One of his first duties was to take part in a lecture tour of Europe and North America. But, between the descent and this tour, he found time back in New Zealand to marry Louise Rose; the circumstances of this will be told in the next chapter. The tour would also serve as their honeymoon.

If Ed needed a reminder that he was part of a team, it came in the form of the £25 per lecture he received on tour with others in the group. At least, it was supposed to be a group affair; by all accounts, Ed's competitiveness came into play here too, and the tour soon evolved into the Ed and George Lowe Show. Ed was the funny man and Lowe the straight man. They may not have been paired to make the assault on the mountain, but they certainly knocked the other bastards off the lecture stage.

'It was all sort of mocking,' says Tom Scott. 'George said he watched Ed change from a moth to a butterfly. He got all this attention and he didn't realise he was funny, but he would say, "I was on a slope. It was a bit dicey, ice was rushing forward and dropping 10,000 feet into Nepal, and I said to myself, 'What do I do here, Ed?' And I said, 'Ed my boy, it's Everest, we better push on."''

It wasn't always like that. Norm Hardie recalls being present with him 'when he gave his first post Everest speech, at a girl's school in Beckenham Kent. He was hesitant, unclear and embarrassed by the adulation'. For someone who grew up shy and insecure, finding you can make a large group of people laugh is the best boost your self-confidence can have. If it comes hard on the heels of an ascent of Everest, you're set.

The tour was not a great money-maker, but it was an excellent reputation-maker. It helped Ed develop the on-stage persona that would serve him so well over the years. He would be self-deprecating, but at the same time never let anyone forget what he had achieved. He would pay courteous credit to those around him—but it was his version of the story that prevailed.

Ed had to wait to tell his own version of the ascent in print until John Hunt's official account had been published. But Ed's book, *High Adventure*, allowed him to pay off his overdraft and start building the house that would be a family home for the rest of his life. It was also the start of a highly successful career as author.

Instant fame, such as Ed experienced, is rare today—and very rare indeed with planned expeditions. The team that went up the mountain, though it certainly made no secret of its existence, did not receive the wall-to-wall media coverage that such an enterprise would attract today, for months before even setting off. A modern equivalent's progress would be documented from inspiration to conclusion with at least a fly-on-the-wall TV series and regular social media updates. Everyone on the team would have been a familiar figure before the final attempt even began. Women's magazines would have asked readers to choose between Team Evans/Bourdillon and Team Hillary/Norgay.

As it was, Ed and Lowe, the larrikins, carried their act over into day-to-day activities—easily, because it wasn't an act. If Ed had to suffer the indignity of an unasked-for knighthood, to be followed by dinner with the Duke of Edinburgh, he was going to have some fun along the way.

In the interests of normalising the whole thing, Ed played up the Kiwi side of his character, specifically contrasting it with the stuffed-shirt Poms on the team: 'When we all went back to the UK, George Lowe and I were the New Zealand members of the party,' he told New Zealand television journalist Mark Sainsbury. 'Every day we were having cocktail parties and champagne and smoked

Scotch salmon and we were meeting lords and ladies. George and I thought it was the funniest thing we had ever experienced in our lives, whereas our fellow members, all very good fellows, took it extremely seriously.'

This down-to-earth quality became a key part of his image, making him beloved of his countrymen who, at that time, still regarded themselves as possessed of an egalitarian spirit. At the same time as he emphasised this, Ed downplayed the un-Kiwi attributes of ambition, ruthlessness and single-mindedness that had got him to this point and that would take him much further.

Ed had to borrow a dinner suit to go to Buckingham Palace. The shirt that came with it had a slit up the back, which nonplussed Ed somewhat; but he was told all would be well as long as he kept his jacket on.

He and George Lowe got ready at a gentlemen's club. Their preparations were handicapped by not knowing where exactly all their new decorations were supposed to go. As Ed typically told the story, he and George spent much time sticking holes in each other in the process of appending their regalia.

As they left to walk to the palace, they were stopped by a photographer from the New Zealand Press Association (NZPA), who was surprised to hear they didn't have a car. But when someone else's Rolls Royce pulled up outside the club and the occupant disappeared inside, the enterprising snapper seized his opportunity: he ordered Ed and George into the car and got his shot.

The aw-shucks persona made it possible for Ed to survive later in the Auckland suburb of Remuera, where he lived. It would have been impossible for him to exist as the global figure he had become if he had acted like one. New Zealanders can only tolerate the ordinary with any comfort, so Ed made himself as ordinary as he could.

And some people mistook apparently ordinary and self-effacing for simple and uncomplicated—notably, to Ed's chagrin, the legendary London journalist Jan Morris who, as James Morris (he later famously changed gender), had provided the first accounts of the conquering of Everest for the *Sunday Times* and who continued over the years to track Ed's career.

'Ed was very offended by Jan Morris every time she said, "What you must understand about Hillary is that he was a very simple man,"' says Tom Scott. 'It made him sound like an amoeba.'

He was not a simple man. He was a complicated man. He was also an intellectual who thought carefully and deeply about things. He had a lot of specialised knowledge that fed into all his work. He knew a lot about mechanics, construction, meteorology, physiology, the sheer science of climbing.

How to top Everest? In the next few years he would be involved in two expeditions—one minor, one major. The first was a disaster. The second was a triumph, but it brought him more criticism than he was ever to bear before or since. And he did not like it.

CHAPTER 4
FAMILY LIFE

The man who had the courage to climb the world's highest mountain could not mount up the courage to ask Louise Mary Rose to marry him. Louise was the daughter of Jim Rose, a lawyer, and his wife, Phyllis—an impressive pair in their own right. An ancestor on the Rose side had been the first mayor of Auckland, and the Roses were stalwarts of the New Zealand mountaineering community, which is how Ed became acquainted with the family.

Ed was soon besotted with the pretty, smart and cultivated Louise, twelve years his junior. A talented musician, Louise had won a scholarship to the Sydney Conservatorium of Music; she arrived there at the end of 1952 to study the viola. Her voice, as heard in old newsreels and family films, has an uncanny similarity to that of Queen Elizabeth II. Such tones aren't in vogue these days, but that was how well brought up young Auckland ladies of the time were taught to speak.

She was not overly enthusiastic about climbing, but she loved the outdoors and had an adventurous spirit that she would have many opportunities to satisfy over the years to come.

That is, if Ed ever got round to asking her to marry him.

Ed always expressed his deepest feelings more comfortably in letters. Those he wrote to Louise are heartfelt and are said, by those who have been lucky enough to read them, to be very moving. But none of these epistles included a proposal of marriage—although many circumlocutions definitely hinted at it, with speculations as to what the future might hold for both of them, and whether the things he hoped for might come to pass.

On his way to the Himalayas and Everest, Ed had stopped off to see Louise in Sydney; and the relationship had got to the point where the pair shared a first kiss. He also stopped off on the way back from England, post-Everest. The local press got wind that Sir Edmund had a girl in town and tried to track her down, with no success.

Ed's account of how Louise came to be his wife changed in the telling over the years. In a deviation from the facts, he wrote in *Nothing Venture, Nothing Win* that he asked Louise to marry him and she agreed. By the time he wrote *View from the Summit* he had revised the story so that, in Sydney after Everest, the two had confirmed that marriage was on the cards, but there was nothing definite.

Back in Auckland, before setting off to the UK for the Everest lecture tour, Ed told Louise's mother Phyl that he wanted to marry her daughter—and would very much like to marry her in time for her to accompany him on the tour, which could then also be a honeymoon. The major obstacle in Ed's mind was one that is common to many men: What if she said no?

Though hardly matinée-idol handsome, Ed was definitely attractive to women. He might have felt more confident of his chances with Louise if he had known the opinion of Earle Riddiford's wife, Rosemary, who, many years later (after her husband's

46

death), confided to Tom Scott: 'Ed was gorgeous . . . Of course, he had no idea how gorgeous he was.'

'They were all remarkable men, weren't they,' said Scott. 'Your husband . . .'

'I wouldn't call Earle remarkable. But Ed—*there* was a man.'

Phyl Rose, who almost certainly knew what her daughter's answer would be, asked Ed if he would like her to ring Louise and ask on his behalf. So, not only was Ed unable to ask his girlfriend to marry him, he couldn't even directly ask her mother to do it for him. But he did accept Phyl's kind offer and, to the surprise of absolutely no one, Louise immediately agreed. In his *HARDtalk* interview Ed ruefully acknowledged that it was 'a cowardly thing on my behalf but it worked out extremely well'.

Louise was one of those rare people about whom no one has a bad word to say. By all accounts, to know her was to love her; and Ed was an extremely lucky man.

'She was just lovely, there is no other way of saying it,' observes John Hillary. 'I truly loved that woman—it was just devastating when she was killed. She was an author, a good wife and a good mum. She was a great aunt, very people orientated, very warm. She was very much like my mother.'

Hilary Carlisle remembers Louise for her kindness and her intuition. 'She was very concerned for others, and was wonderful to me,' says Carlisle. 'I was a 21-year-old, young and naive. She seemed to know what you needed, and nothing ruffled her.'

There were inevitably times when the stresses and strains of a busy life started to show. 'I think she often found it hard,' says son Peter. 'You have this busy household, three kids and she was involved with Volunteer Service Abroad, the Himalayan Trust and her orchestral work. She wrote books, so she had a lot going on.'

Daughter Sarah recalls an occasion when 'Louise had broken her leg and she was stuck in a tent, so she got unusually grumpy, because she usually had such a sunny personality. I remember walking past the tent and she yelled out "Sarah, will you just shut up." She wasn't very happy.'

Ed and Louise's first child, Peter, was born in 1954, followed by Sarah in 1955 and Belinda in 1959. It's an oddity of *Nothing Venture, Nothing Win* that, although Ed notes the occasion of their births, he does not record their names at first mention.

Ed was never going to be a 'hands-on' father, as today's parenting philosophy requires. With Percy as his example, there was little chance of that. He would be involved and active, but in his own way.

'I can't imagine Ed being a great nappy changer in 1954,' says fellow mountaineer and physiologist Mike Gill. 'But he was proud of his kids and loved them, even though he didn't find it easy to show it.' In *View from the Summit*, Ed describes himself as being 'fond' of the children.

Ed and Louise built a home on a property next door to Jim and Phyl Rose, and the grandparents were to have a large presence in the children's lives.

One key to the success of the relationship between Ed and Louise, according to Sarah, was that 'Louise was never fazed by Ed. She thought he was great, but she wasn't afraid of him. She was completely normal with him. She was definitely strong and sometimes feisty, so it was an equal thing, otherwise I think it would have been a disaster, because he was really strong and stroppy.'

'All their married life Louise was the sun and Ed circled around her,' is Tom Scott's description of the dynamic. 'He was in her orbit.'

Their children remember Louise as being able to soften Ed's temper—which could be activated, they say, by several things—

including lethargy, laziness, insolence, and people who didn't stand by their word.

'He did have a fiery temper,' says Sarah, 'but I think Louise modified that a bit and sort of calmed him down. It wasn't so much about his anger but it was needing to be there to calm him down— he had a lot on his plate. Even though he was quite jolly about it, it was stressful. I think it showed that Ed wasn't perfect all the time.'

Nor was he around all the time. His lifestyle meant frequent long absences, notably sixteen months spent away on the Trans-Antarctic Expedition.

'She never moaned,' says Hilary. 'She had the family and she was committed that family life continued, that was the important thing. It was all exciting, she never saw anything as a problem.'

'She went back to her own life,' Sarah explained of her mother's response to Ed's absences. 'She was very busy. She was a writer, a musician and she was heavily involved in the fundraising [for Nepal], so she would give lectures . . . [S]he would just drop everything when Ed came back and help him. But he would go back and she would continue on with her things. The trips she went on with Ed were really important to them . . . if they didn't have that time together, then it wouldn't have been much of a relationship.'

Ed himself said the reason he was able to combine family and a life of adventure was that he had 'a suitable wife. My wife was very long-suffering. She knew that there were certain things I wanted to do and she was happy that I should do them. She was prepared to put up with considerable periods of being alone with the kids.'

Like many an absent father, Ed's approach to discipline was relaxed in the early years of coming and going.

Peter, Sarah and Belinda slipped into the traditional roles that went with the order of their births. Peter was the responsible, serious one of whom most was required. Sarah was the under-the-radar one who got to follow her own path. And Belinda was the pet, adored by everyone.

'She was very like Aunt Louise,' says Hilary of Belinda. 'She had the same personality—the caring side. Peter and Sarah are more Hillarys. The Hillarys are always questioning, always striving to improve or do the best they can. Belinda was fun and always ready for the next thing. She went out of her way to make things work.'

No one who has read Louise's first book, *Keep Calm If You Can*, will forget her description of having to find flowers wherever she went while they were travelling around the United States, because three-year-old Belinda could only go to sleep holding, not a teddy or special blanket, but a fresh flower.

Ed was an inspirational father, to Peter at least. 'I can remember being in Wanaka,' says Peter, 'and Dad would look up and see snow, and you could just feel how it excited him, and I felt the same way. With three kids floating around in the back seat, with Dad whistling and driving, you picked up that emotion. Mum was there, the mountains were sparkling. You knew there was something on his mind and it was all good.'

Even at home, daily life sometimes revolved around adventuring. 'We used to put these little charts together right above the kitchen table,' says Peter. 'Like the next trip. It was either Great Barrier Island, skiing in the South Island, going to Nepal—anywhere really—and we'd tick them off and open another one up.'

'It was always a great adventure when Uncle Ed came to town,' says Hilary, who spent her early years in Norwich in the UK. 'He'd come to London and we'd be taken out of school to drive down and have this amazing day with him . . . wherever he would go, he would take us along.'

When Ed had to attend a function at New Zealand House, in the presence of the likes of New Zealand Prime Minister Keith

Holyoake and soprano Kiri Te Kanawa, he insisted Hilary and her brothers go too. 'We tagged along like country bumpkins. Aunt Louise took us under her wing while Uncle Ed did all the hand-shaking business that he had to.'

Hilary's introduction to Holyoake prompted a misguided attempt at intergenerational humour on his part.

'Oh, have you started social climbing now?' he asked the bewildered twelve-year-old.

Then Uncle Ed just stepped in and sorted it out: 'He always looked after us.' Hilary says she never appreciated Ed's stature—he was just her mum's brother from New Zealand—until she moved to the other side of the world.

John Hillary, Rex's son, was taken along on a family holiday in the South Island. 'Ed loved sporty cars,' John recalls, 'but on that trip he had the Mini Cooper and three kids as well as Aunty Louise. Belinda was that young she sat on her mother's knee all the way in the car.

'He paid for me to fly down and we camped on the bank of the Clutha River. He paid for me and Peter to fly around Mt Aspiring in the aircraft. It was quite amazing.'

One evening John caught a trout that got off the hook. Determined to catch another, he stayed after Ed had gone to bed until he finally landed one at around 9 pm. Thrilled, he ran with this trophy and burst into Ed and Louise's tent to show them.

'Very good, John,' said Ed patiently. Louise told him they would have his fish for breakfast.

'I thought afterwards, maybe it wasn't the best idea to burst into their tent. But they handled it very well.'

Ed had a playful side, and was usually up for horseplay of any description. 'He used to put us in the boot of his Sunbeam Talbot and pretend to drive off with us,' John recalls. 'And when he was having dinner at our house, I would sit beside him. All of a sudden he would turn and say "God, look at that," and when I did and looked back my dinner was gone.'

Sometimes, though, the playfulness turned into a character-building exercise. 'We went deer stalking above a creek and along the hills,' says John. 'When we got near the top of the ridge there was a near vertical strip of about 14 feet which had shelves sticking out. He went up there like a jack rabbit, of course, and disappeared over the top. I had a pack on my back and I got halfway up the darn thing and a piece of shale in my right hand came out of the ground, so I was pivoted on my left foot, by holding on with my left hand, and my pack went all the way around. There I was, looking down . . . and I was thinking, "Oh my God—I am going to die." And my darling uncle, who I loved dearly, leaned over the top and said "Come on, hurry up. What are you doing? Stop messing around." . . . Then he disappeared over the top. So I had no choice but to climb up to join him.'

'My kids loved Ed,' says Mike Gill. 'My daughter Caitlin went to the Himalayas . . . You'd go into a village and he'd receive this huge welcome and she would be able to sit alongside Ed and feel so important.'

Louise shared the adventurous spirit. In 1962 the opportunity arose to take everyone to the US for a year. They would be based in Chicago, and Ed would travel around lecturing to the staff of the World Book Encyclopedia, which promoted itself as 'the number-one selling print encyclopedia in the world' and was the most important rival of the more famous Encyclopaedia Britannica. They would also tour National Forest Campgrounds and report on them for the US Department of Agriculture; and they travelled as far as Alaska, testing camping gear for Sears Roebuck.

In *Keep Calm If You Can*, the conqueror of Everest is seen as a mere mortal, struggling with the normal vicissitudes of a family camping holiday: forgetting to pack the right map; taking his eyes off the road to deal with his misbehaving kids in the back seat; leading the fun charge with sing-alongs in the car; and retelling the Jimmy Job stories his own father made up to entertain him.

But it is Louise—typically for the time—who does most of the parenting. At the end of their trip home, they arrive in Nepal, where Ed takes Peter and Sarah for a two-day trek, complete with Sherpas, into the mountains. Louise stays behind with Belinda, who is unwell. The highlight comes when the Hillarys reach a point that provides Peter and Sarah with an inspiring view across Nepal to Mt Everest.

The childhood treks and trips were frequent—scaled down so the children could manage them easily, and with copious supplies of chocolate to keep spirits up. 'And when we were really young,' says Peter, 'if we were having a hard time, we would be bound into a sleeping bag and dropped into a basket on a Sherpa's back.'

'It was quite hard going overseas,' recalls Sarah. 'People barely travelled in those days. It was a major deal when we went to Nepal because they had to save money, and there was a lot of organisation.'

In *Keep Calm*, Louise reports Ed telling her that if the whole family was to make a trip to the Himalayas she would need to produce another book to finance it. It's not entirely clear from her account whether he was joking or not; but Mike Gill also describes her having to 'write books to subsidise their trips to the Himalayas'.

Whatever the motivation, Louise produced another fine family memoir in *A Yak for Christmas*, the story of the family's trip to Nepal, India and elsewhere. 'The trips to Nepal were amazing,' says Peter. 'On one, Mum took us across India to Nepal when the whole country was in lock-down. There were military police everywhere and she had this gaggle of children.'

'First we were turned back to Sydney,' says Sarah. 'They decided the planes couldn't go through. Then I managed to leave my passport behind. They held the plane, so when I got to the airport I was thrown into a jeep, driven across the tarmac and came on board. I was totally oblivious to the whole thing except my mother was crying and all the other passengers were glaring at me.'

One less tense, but no less adventurous, jaunt was to the challenging environment of central Australia, following the Birdsville Track. 'And there was this tremendous one-in-ten-year massive flood,' says Sarah. 'It happened when we were camped in the loop of a river. We were in the tent and the parents were in a campervan, so they rescued us in the middle of the night . . . When we woke up the next morning there was a raging torrent around us, we had to try and get through that with the car. They took the fan belt off so we could drive through, but as soon as we got over it we discovered there were entire lakes of water and it was really hard to get out.'

As his absences grew fewer and shorter, and the children got older—more visible and less biddable—Ed began to have a more direct, day-to-day involvement in raising them.

'Parents of his generation,' says Peter, 'were on a cusp. There had been a way of raising children, probably for a hundred years, up to that point, where it might have started bending to the sort of new age way of doing things.

'He would try and make us do what his father did, which was really strict. He did move towards [the new way], but I do think it was the way that previous generation had been.'

Louise, who was younger than Ed, tended to prefer the new style of parenting. Sarah thinks Louise found all the usual faults in children—answering back, not cleaning their rooms—easier to deal with because she had spent more time with them.

Ed had firm views about money. He was not wealthy—though far from poor—and if the children wanted anything out of the ordinary they had to work to earn the money to pay for it.

As for bringing boys home . . . 'That was a little bit difficult,' says Sarah. 'Ed was very old-fashioned when it came to me. It was very different for Peter. I was the oldest girl and Ed was very protective. I remember being invited to a party and being told at the last minute I couldn't go. I don't know what they thought I was going to do but I remember our grandparents coming over to comfort me about the whole thing because it was so embarrassing.'

On another occasion, Sarah had arranged to have a party in the garage, which had been especially decorated for the occasion. But when someone rang and told Ed a large group of people were planning to gatecrash it, he told Sarah the party was cancelled.

'So I had to ring everyone—that was total humiliation. I told Ed he had to tell me who it was [who had called], but by the time he got around to it he couldn't remember. He was very strict about socialising and things and that was one of the reasons why I left home really early and went to Dunedin University. I left school after the sixth form, went down there and partied up.'

Just as Ed was having to learn how to be 'Ed Hillary', his children were learning how to be 'Ed Hillary's kids'. Being the child of a celebrity was rare at that time, especially in New Zealand. 'The one thing I remember is, it was really embarrassing when they asked you what your father did and I never knew what that really was with Ed,' says Sarah.

'He was the beginning of this new era,' says Peter. 'Job descriptions are really complicated, varied and different these days. Back then, without a traditional job, it didn't mean you weren't hugely successful and very innovative and clever ... Dad was something else.'

'I always felt I could never talk about my family like most other people would . . .' says Sarah. 'I always felt that, if I said something, everyone was listening, so you couldn't make casual comments. They will take it away and it will be their "Ed Hillary story".'

One of the few things Peter and Sarah disagree about when discussing their upbringing is whether their paternity earned them any special treatment. Sarah thinks not: 'I don't think we were treated differently, but we did have different experiences. At school, I was just a normal person with my friends, but we would meet other people who would come and visit Ed, then we went on trips that perhaps other people didn't have the chance to do so we did have different experiences.'

'I remember being a small boy at school,' says Peter, 'and going with [Governor-General Sir Bernard] Fergusson's son back to Government House and playing, and Mum coming to pick me up and curtseying to Lady Fergusson. Later in India, when I was 30, I had lunch with Indira Gandhi and carried on up to see Tenzing. They are not typical experiences.'

As for school, Peter says there was no sense of different treatment by the teachers, but there was from the students. 'I remember walking around the quadrangle, where students weren't meant to walk, and these kids yelled out: "You just think you can do that just because you are the son of Ed Hillary." So I personally felt a lot of that.'

The greatest pressure was the need to perform for the media. 'Whenever there was a photo opportunity we had to smile for the camera,' says Sarah. 'Already when we were very young we had to deal with a public and private division. I remember having a tantrum as a small child when Ed had come back from some trip. I was very tiny but I refused to smile.'

Sarah was not keen on heights—like her mother, she liked mountains, not mountaineering. Instead, she found her calling as an art conservator, becoming principal conservator at Auckland Art Gallery and exhibiting as an artist in her own right.

Ed wanted all three children to go to university and become professionals. He was enthusiastic about Peter studying engineering—but instead he studied geology for a while, before abandoning it. Peter says: 'He was incredibly proud of what Sarah achieved with her career and her qualifications, which he felt was a real triumph and so do I. Belinda was really interested in medicine and I think she would have been a fantastic doctor.'

Peter, on the other hand, would follow in his father's footsteps.

Over all the ups and downs of childhood, Louise's benevolent presence cast a warm glow. 'Our mother was a sunny personality,' says Sarah, 'a very positive person. She could also be very cynical and very funny, but she basically looked on the bright side, and she liked people a lot. She was very outgoing.'

Sarah once got a letter from a man who recalled meeting Ed and Louise, not long after they got married. 'He said Louise entertained them all evening. There were lots of laughs and wonderful stories. Ed just sat back and enjoyed the whole experience. He felt they were so obviously in love.'

'I think that, from the five of us,' says Peter, 'Sarah and I and Dad were of a certain strong-willed ilk, reasonably complex personalities, determined. Our younger sister was very much like my mother. They were both incredibly capable people, they were much more adept at dealing with people and knew how to weave their way around things, and really for our family they were the glue that made it function. They could bond it all together and make it work.'

Bonding it together and making it work was something Ed would struggle to do in years to come.

CHAPTER 5
TO THE END OF THE EARTH

When Ed reached the top of Everest, his career as a mountaineer could be said to have peaked. There were still many more unscaled mountains to climb, alpine challenges that men had been dreaming about for years—some reputed to be even more difficult than Everest. But several circumstances would keep Ed from another success like Everest.

His health was a major factor—that apparently superhuman constitution was not invulnerable after all. The outcome of his first post-Everest mountaineering challenge was a portent of things to come. In 1954, having gained permission from the Nepalese Government, the New Zealand Alpine Club chose Ed—and who else could they possibly have chosen?—to lead a Himalayan expedition into the Barun Valley. Among its peaks were two that would loom large in Ed's story in years to come: the unclimbed Makalu and Ama Dablam. Members of the expedition included Everest veterans Charles Evans and George Lowe, as well as Norm Hardie, Bill Beaven and others. Among the Sherpas was Mingma Tsering, whose life would become closely connected with Ed's until Tsering's death in 1993.

Having set up base camp, Ed sent two groups off on surveying sorties while he, along with Jim McFarlane and Brian Wilkins, headed off to explore the Barun Glacier. Ed returned after three days of the planned four-day trip, while McFarlane and Wilkins pressed on.

As the hour when they were due to return came and went, and then more time passed, Ed was beginning to worry. Finally, an exhausted Wilkins came into view. He and McFarlane had fallen into a crevasse; Wilkins had managed to extricate himself but McFarlane was injured and was still trapped there.

Ed returned to the site with some Sherpas. He tied a rope around his chest and had himself lowered to the injured man. But the chest was the wrong place to take such weight and, although he didn't realise it at the time, he cracked three ribs. Numerous attempts to lift McFarlane out failed, and it was all Ed could do to get himself out.

It was clear McFarlane couldn't be removed that night, so sleeping bags were thrown down to him. Although he told his would-be rescuers he had got into the bags, he had merely wrapped them around himself and would pay the price later with the loss of parts of his feet and fingers to frostbite.

Eventually McFarlane was brought to safety, but this wasn't to be the end of the expedition. A party set out to attempt Makalu, leaving the injured Ed behind. But his restlessness proved his undoing and, although in pain, he set off to join the party.

Before long his injuries got the better of him: in addition to his broken ribs, he suffered a recurrence of the malaria he had contracted during the war. He began to hallucinate—and he in turn had to be carried out. George Lowe worried Ed might die, and John Hunt was asked to write an obituary—just in case.

Norm Hardie is scathing in his assessment of what happened. 'There were lots of mountain technical mistakes and leadership omissions . . . His lack of language to explain to Sherpas on the surface what was to be done. Taking all his big weight on just a chest loop was forcing big stress on his body and making it difficult to extract himself at the top of the crevasse lip. Not going down the full length of rope, and then removing his crampons and putting McFarlane into his sleeping bag. Among mountaineers there was dismay to learn that the man who had climbed Everest was so lacking in mountain skills.'

On the other hand, McFarlane, who was the person with most reason to be critical, bore the expedition leader no ill will in later years: 'I feel privileged to have known him,' he told Pat Booth.

After the Barun Valley expedition, Ed slowed down; he even went back to helping Rex with the beekeeping. There was still time for the occasional mountain, though. With Harry Ayres, he made the first successful attempt of Mt Magellan in the South Island in 1955.

Ed had got into the habit of adventure. It kept at bay a tendency to melancholia that Louise recognised was never far from the surface and that would erupt if Ed didn't have something exciting to do.

His next adventure would occupy him for the next couple of years, and preoccupy him for a lot longer. The 1955–58 Commonwealth Trans-Antarctic Expedition (TAE) is still the most controversial exploit in Ed's career.

The Antarctic had irresistible appeal for Ed. Ernest Shackleton and the other early explorers in the region had been among his greatest childhood heroes. At the time of the TAE, Shackleton had been dead just over 30 years. But perhaps the great age of polar exploration was not over. Perhaps it just needed a kick along.

British geologist Dr Vivian Fuchs was planning to cross the Antarctic from the Weddell Sea, with two objectives in mind. The primary aim—serious and scientific—was to conduct a geological survey to find out, in layman's terms, what was under the ice. Along the way, he would be the first person to cross the great southern continent on land: the British press called it the 'last great journey in the world'.

To achieve his goal, Fuchs needed many things—not least, money. The name of the conqueror of Everest would definitely help with that. He would also need supplies dropped at certain points so his party would have enough fuel and food to get them through. Ed could come in handy there too.

The plan was for a British base—called Shackleton Base—to be established first, on the Weddell Sea. A New Zealand base—Scott Base—would then be established on the Ross Sea on the other side of Antarctica. Fuchs and company would set off from Shackleton Base; and Ed and the New Zealand support party would set out from Scott Base and travel roughly halfway to the South Pole, leaving supplies in depots that they would establish along the way.

As we know, Ed liked to be first, and the expedition as proposed didn't seem to offer much scope for firsts. But no one had reached the South Pole by land since Scott in 1912, and he would be heading that way. Also, no one had ever got there by vehicle. Ed held out hope for some time that there would be a separate New Zealand expedition, which, naturally, he would lead; and he kept his options open. But his hopes came to nothing and he eventually accepted the 'junior' role and became deputy leader of the TAE.

He did his bit back home, barnstorming the country, addressing fundraising meetings and cajoling donations from schoolchildren and others. The public could even buy 'shares' in the expedition, in the form of garish certificates.

Fuchs invited Ed to accompany him on the trip to set up the British base so that Ed could get some Antarctic experience. But the expedition got off to a near-disastrous start on the Weddell Sea side in 1955. Fuchs made a bad call in deciding what route to follow. When the captain of their ship, the *Theron*, questioned the choice, Fuchs overrode him. As a result, the *Theron* was nearly iced in. Only the superlative flying of New Zealand Wing Commander John Claydon, who managed a daring take-off from the ice and found an escape route for the *Theron* from the air, allowed the team to find a way out.

Because of poor planning, much of the team's gear was flooded; and when the *Theron* was finally able to get out, after being delayed for a month, it had to do so in such a hurry that the hut being built for the men who were to remain behind over the winter was not finished. This meant the men spent the coldest Antarctic months in a packing crate by day, and sleeping in tents by night.

Ed was aghast. Summing up the near-disaster on the *Theron*, he said it had given him as much experience in negotiating pack ice as he would ever be likely to need. In *Nothing Venture, Nothing Win*, after having described in excruciating detail Fuchs's series of blunders, Ed concluded drily by expressing admiration for his leader's continued belief in his own decision-making skills.

As for Fuchs's attitude to Ed, from the very start the Englishman had shown the lofty contempt that would permanently sour relations between the two men. He seemed to grasp every opportunity to patronise Ed. As far as Dr Fuchs was concerned, Sir Edmund was the junior partner—a glorified grocery boy in charge of some deliveries.

A key difference between the two, as Ed had noted, was that Fuchs was a man who stuck with his plan, come ice or high water. Ed was also a meticulous planner, but he could change his plan in an instant if he saw that the circumstances required it.

Fuchs went so far as to exclude Ed—his deputy leader—from planning meetings, telling him he was just along as an observer. Ed was even shut out of social occasions. When the captain of the Royal Navy vessel the *Protector*, which was in the vicinity and kept in contact with the *Theron*, invited Fuchs to bring a group on board for dinner, the scientist excluded Ed. When an invitation was extended to the rest of the team to come over for a drink, the captain was mortified to encounter the Conqueror of Everest and to realise he hadn't been included in the first party.

'I don't think Fuchs had thought it through properly,' says Mike Gill now, looking back at Fuchs's treatment of Ed. 'If you are dealing with someone as famous as that, with that personality, they just don't do as they are told.'

Seeing Fuchs botch one decision after another convinced Ed to make his own arrangements. This extended from the gear everyone wore (Fuchs went for a one-size-fits-all approach, while Ed ensured that everything was made to fit the man who would wear it) to the music (Fuchs limited listening time so there wouldn't be squabbles).

After he returned to New Zealand, to prepare for his part in the expedition Ed took his team to the Tasman Glacier for practice in conditions that were as near-Antarctic as he could find. And he chose his men for characteristically canny—if apparently quixotic—reasons. Faced with a choice of two potential radio officers, for instance, he chose the one who didn't call him 'sir' during his interview—naval captain Peter Mulgrew.

New Zealand's contribution of items for the expedition was loaded onto the *Endeavour*, and the contingent set sail in December 1956. Peter Mulgrew's wife, June, who, along with Louise and Peter, was farewelling the team, described a slight awkwardness when the wharfside band had to keep playing 'Now is the Hour' as the tide pushed the boat back to port.

Even before leaving New Zealand, Ed had pondered the possibility of going to the Pole on a frolic of his own. It's not clear exactly when he made his final decision to travel the extra 800 kilometres past Depot 700—the point 700 miles from Scott Base that had been agreed on as the official finishing point for his supply drop-offs. Fuchs's high-handedness alone would not have been enough to make up Ed's mind, but it would have contributed. 'What started as a calculated whim became a steely master plan,' in Tom Scott's words.

'Ed never did things on the spur of the moment,' said Ed's brother Rex. 'He would have done some planning.'

As had happened on the *Theron* trip, Fuchs, carrying out his time-consuming and exacting task, started to fall behind almost before he set out. Meanwhile Ed's party, on the way to establishing Depot 700, managed to explore some previously unknown areas of the continent and do experiments of their own. But Ed was still left with a lot of time on his hands, and he wasn't of a mind to slow his pace to match Fuchs's, sluggish progress.

And so began the story of the so-called Race to the Pole—which was never really a race because Fuchs was never actually in it; but, with one explorer approaching the Pole from one direction and another from the other direction, it did have elements of a race about it.

Both parties had air support, and messages were carried back and forth by this means as well as through radio contact, which also kept them in touch with the outside world. As the news filtered through, the newspapers in Britain and New Zealand reacted along patriotic lines: Britain accused Ed of exceeding his brief and grandstanding for personal glory rather than putting the empire first; and labelled Ed the 'Abominable Showman'. In New Zealand, the general reaction could best be summed up in the idiom 'Whack-oh the diddle-oh'. It looked like their boy was going to do it again.

In *Nothing Venture, Nothing Win*, Ed records an argument with himself about whether or not to push on that would have done Hamlet proud. In the end, he says, he decided to go because, if he hadn't, he would have hated himself for it. He went, in other words, because it was there.

Ed has it both ways in the documentary *A View from the Top*— he says that he discovered 'later Fuchs wanted to be the first person to bring a vehicle to the South Pole. I wasn't aware of this, and if I had been maybe we wouldn't have pushed on. But on the other hand, maybe we would have pushed on.'

His rival, for his part, went to his grave denying any interest in being first to the Pole. 'It was nothing to do with me who got there first,' Fuchs said years later, in the same documentary. 'It wasn't a race. I'm a man of science. I was interested in science. I wasn't interested in the glory of getting there first.'

Ed's son and daughter have their own view of the journey to the Pole. 'The media made it into a race,' says Peter. 'It wasn't a race. He is just a driven person. He wanted to go to the Pole. Even to this day it is hard to do anything in Antarctica, and back then it was desperately difficult, so if you get an opportunity like that, you know . . .'

'And I think he got sick of being bossed around,' says Sarah. 'They were pretty condescending.'

'He wouldn't have liked being bossed, because he always liked to be boss,' Peter adds.

Ed was clearly setting up his depots and leaving supplies at a speed that would leave him a large comfort zone in which to reach the South Pole long before Fuchs.

A series of messages were sent—misheard, misunderstood or ignored—flying between London, New Zealand and points in Antarctica. Anything suggesting that they slow down was ignored by Ed, albeit with an appearance of giving due consideration, before he went ahead and did what he was always going to do.

Eventually Ed had the last word: 'I am hell-bent for the South Pole—God willing and crevasses permitting.'

John Claydon was flying regularly between the New Zealand support party and Scott Base, supporting Ed himself with reconnaissance from the air and delivering fuel supplies. He was one of the first to be let in on the semi-secret. 'John, I want to tell you something confidentially,' said Ed. 'I am planning to head to the Pole. Do you have enough aviation fuel to fly in extra supplies to further depots?'

More fuel would be needed than originally planned, in order to get Ed to the Pole and leave enough to supply the Fuchs party.

'Hell, no!' was Claydon's response. But when he got back to Scott Base, he asked British oil company and expedition sponsor, BP, to supply an extra 20 drums of the fuel they had formulated especially for the conditions.

And he approached US Rear Admiral George Dufek, stationed with the American Antarctic program at McMurdo Sound, who agreed to transport the fuel on a US ship. The drums were sent as deck cargo, but they came loose and ended up going overboard.

Claydon, who was also flying in telegrams telling Ed to slow down, found himself in a tangled web, and so he rang Dufek: 'Look, that fuel you sent—it all went overboard.'

'Well, John, what are you going to do now?'

'Well, it's a hell of a situation and I hate to say it—what's the chance of flying it down?'

'John, that's a pretty tall order isn't it?'

A week later Claydon got a message from air headquarters asking why he had made a personal request to BP. His report must have been adequate, as he heard no more about it. And thanks to

Dufek's cooperation, another 20 drums were flown in. Without Claydon's initiative, Ed wouldn't have got to the Pole.

Not everyone in Ed's group wanted to continue past Depot 700—the agreed-upon finishing point, after which they were supposed to return to Scott Base. Only Mulgrew was particularly keen. Engineer Murray Ellis was most reluctant, but Ed was insistent—he had to be, as he could not afford to go without the engineer. They faced off and Ellis ultimately backed down.

Some say Ed bullied his men into it. Others that he cajoled them. Whichever explanation you accept, there is no denying that not all of them wanted to go, but they went.

Team member and fellow New Zealander, Jim Bates, wasn't worried about upsetting the expedition organisers—he was worried about dying. Ed wanted to go in a straight line. 'It was too dangerous,' Bates told the NZ *Sunday Star-Times* in 2000. 'There were crevasses everywhere. It made us uptight. We put our foot down and said "We go west". If Ed had disagreed, that would have been it. We would have gone back. After that we got on well as a team.

'There was quite a bit of friction and tension. Conditions were far from safe. It got to the point that it was something like the Mutiny on the Bounty. We told Ed that unless we were all involved in the decision-making we would turn back. We would have too. He was hurt. No doubt about that. But he had no choice.'

John Claydon wasn't surprised that Ed got his way. 'It was that determination that took him to Everest,' he says. 'No question about it. He wasn't a normal person in that respect. If he had made up his mind to do a thing, he would do it and nobody could do a thing about it.'

Claydon also observes that Ed's failure to be selected for pilot training and subsequent training in navigation in the air force was a factor in his success at the Pole.

'On the Polar Plateau you are in the wilderness,' says Claydon. 'There are no landmarks, but he was able to navigate. He may have brushed up on his astronomical navigation before he went south. You see, down there in the wilderness you don't even know where south is. If you are in the wilderness like the Polar Plateau and there is nothing to see anywhere, where would you go? You can only do that by taking sun shots and you have to use navigation tables and all the rest of it. I have copies of his plans of the route he did. It is a very complicated business. So if he had become a pilot and had lived to tell the tale, he wouldn't have learnt the navigational skills to get to the South Pole.'

The party was riding on tractors, which progressed in single file, roped together so that if one fell into a crevasse the others would provide an anchor. The group rotated the risky task of being lead tractor driver—that is, first into the crevasse—among themselves.

The tractors are a big part of this story. Ed used them not just to get to the Pole, but to develop his technique of playing down his achievements in order to highlight them. That the journey was made on Massey Ferguson tractors is repeatedly mentioned in all accounts. The impression given is that on the way to Antarctica he stopped off at the farm and picked up a couple of tractors from the shed. In truth, he had visited Massey Ferguson's British headquarters and researched the vehicles and their capabilities thoroughly before setting out.

Doug McKenzie, the official press correspondent travelling with the party, had originally been keen on continuing; but then he began to have doubts and opted to fly back to Scott Base. There he encountered others with doubts about Ed's plan, including one anonymous team member who said, 'There are three expeditions going on here. There's the British Commonwealth Trans-Antarctic

Expedition, the New Zealand Antarctic Expedition, and Hillary's private fucking expedition to the Pole.'

McKenzie's unusually harsh assessment of Ed, no doubt formulated in the midst of an icy wasteland, was expanded upon in his book *Opposite Poles* (1963): 'Hillary was principally concerned about Hillary. Behind his easy-going manner he held that threat of ruthlessness which must be possessed in some degree by all successful leaders. With a casualness which was startling to those who met it, he was willing to place members of his party temporarily on the sideline if this became necessary for his major purpose.'

Ed remained oblivious to any whispers of the controversy raging back home and beyond. New Zealand Prime Minister Walter Nash commissioned a report on whether or not he should intervene: he was told there were insufficient grounds, and that such a move would be most unpopular with the voters.

Ed reached the Pole on 4 January 1958, with little fuel to spare, but fifteen days ahead of his expedition leader. The news of Ed's arrival was heralded laconically in the *Auckland Star*, which managed to include a backhanded swipe at Fuchs:

Hillary scores his second triumph
NZ Party reaches Pole;
Dr Fuchs expected there tomorrow.

Back in London, Buckingham Palace got in touch with the TAE committee. It appeared the Queen had heard the news and wanted to know what might be appropriate. Should she make some acknowledgement or send congratulations to her knight?

'Under no circumstances,' came the thunderous reply.

Ed and his party were flown back to Scott Base, where they awaited Fuchs's eventual arrival at the Pole. At that point, Ed was flown back so as to guide them for the rest of the return

TO THE END OF THE EARTH

journey—not unlike a father having to go out late at night to retrieve an errant teenager.

There are still people who are violently exercised by Ed's decision to go to the Pole—and his success. The key complaint seems to be insubordination. Fuchs was the boss. Ed had a job to do and should have stopped when he had done it, rather than exceed his job description.

But while he may have resorted to some subterfuge in planning his scheme, and some aggressive leadership in persuading his men to carry it out, Ed did not interfere with Fuchs's plans. Fuchs completed his geological survey and became the first person to cross the Antarctic continent on land. If that achievement has been overshadowed by Ed's, then that is because Ed casts a longer shadow.

Pat Booth describes this assessment as 'very tolerant. I wonder what Ed's attitude would have been if he had been aiming to scale Everest from the south face and there had been a team put in to make supply dumps and one had gone on to make the ascent. He would not have been amused.'

Official footage shows the two explorers greeting each other with the most cordial of handshakes. In fact, Fuchs could not afford to be seen to resent Ed: only by holding himself in check could he hope to silence, or at least mute, any of the many legitimate criticisms of Fuchs's performance that Ed could make.

Ed delighted in telling the story of how, as the party now made its way to Scott Base, Fuchs forced him to sit in the back, where cold and boredom were his companions. Every so often, however, the party would stop and Ed would have to be let out so he could look around and tell them in which direction they should be going.

Somehow Ed and Fuchs managed to coauthor a book on the expedition, from their very different perspectives. But Ed was

71

personally stung by the criticism that came his way. Over the years he would reveal an abundant ability to dish it out, but less of a knack for taking it.

'I tried to infer it didn't affect me,' he said. 'It did. I didn't like all the hullabaloo. It was the first time I'd struck unfavourable publicity about something of this nature. On my return I went to ground for quite a while. It was the last time I did any beekeeping.'

Significantly, he was not invited to celebrations for the tenth anniversary of the expedition—although he was invited to the twenty-fifth and the fiftieth anniversaries. And Fuchs managed to find one final way to annoy Ed, who was, if not quite a prude, conservative in his attitudes to personal relationships. When the two men went on a speaking tour of South Africa together, Fuchs was accompanied by a woman when he greeted Ed: 'Ed, you've met my wife?'

Indeed he had, but this wasn't her. Ed knew full well that the woman he was greeting was Fuchs's former secretary. Ed's sense of honour precluded pretending that people were who they were not, but for once he went with Fuchs's plan and played along.

'I was a bit annoyed actually,' he later told Tom Scott.

CHAPTER 6
TRIPLE PEAK

Most of Ed's classic adventuring occurred in a relatively short period, between Everest in 1953 and the Himalayan Scientific and Mountaineering Expedition (HSME) of 1960–61. This last would indirectly lead to what Ed considered his greatest achievement—his work in Nepal through the Himalayan Trust.

The HSME was also known as the Silver Hut Expedition because of the futuristic-looking hut, like a giant drainpipe coated in aluminium paint, that was built to provide shelter for the party while they wintered at 5791 metres before attempting the assault on 8481-metre Makalu, the world's fifth-highest mountain.

This was three expeditions in one: a hunt for the yeti; a physiological study of existence at high altitudes; and another attempt to climb Makalu, this time without oxygen (the French had summited Makalu with oxygen in 1955).

Ed had already discussed with physiologist and Everest veteran Griffith Pugh the possibility of spending a long time at high altitude to measure the effects on the human body—and also to see whether, over a long time, the body would adapt and learn to survive with less oxygen. This would, of course, be a precursor to an eventual attempt to climb Everest without supplementary oxygen—one of Ed's list of firsts that he was still hoping to knock off.

It was a major enterprise, another long expedition, planned to take place in the nine months between monsoon seasons. It was also a media event: world-famous zoologist Marlin Perkins, host of the popular American TV show *Animal Kingdom*, joined the team. As team member Desmond Doig—a Calcutta-based journalist who co-wrote with Ed an entertaining account, *High in the Thin Cold Air*—explained, it was the first Himalayan adventure Ed had been involved in that counted what he called 'arty types' among its personnel. Ed's definition of arty types included journalists and makers of television programs.

There are several anecdotes concerning the background to this expedition. According to Peter Mulgrew, Ed wanted to scale Everest from the northern side.

The initial spark occurred in 1959, which was also the year in which Ed and Louise's third child, Belinda, was born; and when he travelled to Chicago to make a short film for the publishers of the World Book Encyclopedia—the start of a long and happy working relationship with this company. Ed's affable Kiwi-bloke persona was a character the Americans had not encountered before; and his modest appearance—and financial requirements to match—went down a treat with the corporates.

In conversation with the company's PR director, John Dienhart, Ed outlined his plan for an expedition with a physiological bent. According to some, he threw in the idea of a yeti hunt on the spot, to spice it up a bit. Dienhart was very keen and Ed suddenly found himself with a sponsor.

Another explanation of the background to the expedition was the official view of the Soviet Union, as outlined by one I Andropov, a foreign affairs official: 'Sir Edmund took rocket experts from New Zealand and the United States on the expedition which was financed by the United States Air Force. He was more interested in spying on China than looking for the abominable snowman.'

'As uninterested' might have been a fairer description. It is most unlikely that practical, pragmatic, hard-nosed and -headed Ed ever believed the yeti (or the Abominable Snowman) existed—even though Eric Shipton counted himself among the believers. But many of Ed's Nepali friends and acquaintances were convinced they had encountered such a creature; some even when they were not under the influence of chang, the local alcoholic beverage. However, he was canny enough to know that this romantic quest would attract attention and money.

Ed assembled a particularly talented group, mixing old hands such as Griffith Pugh, Norm Hardie, Michael Ward and Peter Mulgrew with enthusiastic youngsters such as Mike Gill. Gill had been enthralled by Ed since before Everest, and had been at a talk Ed and George Lowe had given about their time on the Shipton reconnaissance expedition. He later became a lifelong friend and colleague of Ed's.

The inherent flaw in the yeti hunt was that Ed was setting out to test the existence of something that wasn't there—trying to prove a negative. However, although there were no yetis, there was plenty of evidence that yetis existed, available at a price. As Pat Booth put it, the team failed to find a yeti but they discovered a yeti industry. They passed up the offer of a yeti skeleton on the grounds that it was that of a dog. Yeti fur frequently came their way, but nearly always turned out to be that of a blue bear.

Some monasteries held sacred yeti relics. One, at Khumjung, was home to a yeti scalp, which Ed and some of his party were not just shown but were allowed to try on. Eventually they negotiated to borrow this scalp and take it abroad for testing. After a grand tour of laboratories in Chicago, Paris and London it was proved to be a fake made from the hair of the goat-like serow—albeit a couple of centuries old.

That left only the question of explaining away numerous sightings of footprints unlike those of any known creature; these were what had convinced Shipton. Some prints were reputed to show a toe perpendicular to the main part of the foot, which seemed inexplicable until this deformity was noted in Sherpa feet. Others were simply too big for any creature that lived in the area. Ed eventually employed cool logic to show that these prints were the result of a smaller creature's prints that the sun had melted and merged into one. Now, perhaps, they could get on with their expedition and more productive research.

Those in the Silver Hut spent their time working and training— there was a lot of stationary bike riding with a splendid view of Ama Dablam, as yet unclimbed.

Ed had been in New Zealand organising supplies, and was en route from Kathmandu when four of his team achieved the first summiting of this mountain's 6856-metre peak. Unfortunately, permission to make the attempt had been neither sought from, nor granted by, the Nepalese Government, which had grown increasingly firm about the need for outsiders to seek permission to climb its mountains. This was a body so pernickety it maintained a time difference of ten minutes with neighbouring India.

The Nepalese were not pleased. Permission to climb Makalu was withdrawn and the Himalayan Scientific and Mountaineering Expedition of 1960–61 was told to leave the country.

Ed says in *High in the Thin Cold Air* that he was astonished that this group had attempted Ama Dablam—a claim that seems more than a little disingenuous. He knew full well that with time on their hands—and the researchers had everything well under control on the scientific side of things—there is really only one thing fit young mountaineers will do in the vicinity of a magnificent, unclimbed mountain. It would be like putting an ambitious, competitive man in a direct line to the South Pole and telling him to stop halfway there.

The government had spoken, however. So Ed had to turn around and go back to the low altitude of Kathmandu, where he spent several frustrating days as an unwilling participant in a game of bureaucratic musical chairs. Eventually, on payment of a not particularly extortionate sum, permission to attempt Makalu was given.

This, after all, was what most of the previous year had been about—preparing a team at high altitude for an attempt without oxygen on the fifth highest mountain in the world. It was a great mountaineering challenge. However, not long into the attempt, Ed showed the first signs of altitude sickness. He decided not to go past 6460 metres. Four days later, with no improvement, he went lower again. There was still no improvement; on the contrary, when he woke up the next morning he was unable to speak properly. Ed had suffered a small stroke.

Michael Ward assessed him and instructed him to stay below 4570 metres, which effectively meant he was no longer in control of his own mission. Ward took over. Pugh wanted Ed to return as low as Kathmandu, but he was determined to oversee the school building project he had started at Khumjung. He also turned down offers from Peter Mulgrew and Mingma Tsering to stay back with him. Eventually he was well enough to undertake the 15-day walk out of the area.

So the assault on Makalu continued without Ed. On 17 May a group of Sherpas nearly perished when one fell and the five roped to him fell with him. Only two, including Tsering, were injured, and they were sent back. The others continued as far as 8320 metres before leaving Peter Mulgrew, Tom Nevison and Annullu, a Sherpa, ready for a final attempt.

Then, heartbreakingly close to the summit, Mulgrew collapsed in great pain, struggling to breathe. He had suffered a pulmonary embolism—a blocked artery—in his right arm. This might have been enough to kill him in his garden in Auckland; at 120 metres from the top of Makalu, the outlook could hardly be bleaker—especially when it became clear that Annullu was also in pain with a cracked rib. Nevertheless the Sherpa went for help, and water, oxygen and a tent reached Mulgrew.

There was no radio contact between Mulgrew's group and anyone else, but eventually word got to the others. The attempt on Makalu was now in tatters, with men spread across the mountain at various camps in various states of ill health, injury and exhaustion. Slowly, painfully and against all odds Peter Mulgrew was brought down from Makalu. He was alive, but in appalling shape.

It would be almost another twenty years before anyone managed to climb Makalu without oxygen.

Ed was greatly disappointed by the outcome of this expedition—the worst of any he had been involved in, even though, miraculously, no lives were lost. It seems clear that what befell him on the mountain was the direct result of his trip to regain permission for the attempt. After spending so long at a relatively low level, he had not had time to readjust to the higher altitude before the climb began. He continued to believe that if he had been able to stay in charge, the outcome would have been much better—especially for Peter Mulgrew.

Some good came out of the expedition. Griffith Pugh published the results of the expedition's research in the *British Medical Journal* in 1962. His conclusion stated: 'The party appeared to acclimatize well to 19,000 ft. (5,790 m.), and card-sorting and other psychological tests revealed no evidence of mental impairment. However, all members of the party continued to lose weight, and this makes it doubtful if they could have stayed there indefinitely. Newcomers on Mt. Makalu, after four to six weeks' acclimatization, were, if anything, fitter and more active than men who had wintered at 19,000 ft. (5,790 m.).' Another of the physiologists on the trip, Jim Milledge, wrote in *High Altitude Medicine and Biology*, 'Many of the findings were not repeated for many years, and none has been refuted.'

In his own summary of what was learnt about high-altitude existence, Ed noted that any gains achieved by habituation to low levels of oxygen were offset because it was so difficult to exercise in that state; this meant that keeping in climb-ready physical shape proved impossible.

As had happened on other occasions, Ed's leadership was called into question in the wake of what happened at Makalu. It's not easy to lead when you've just had a stroke, and there's no way of knowing whether Ed's certainty that things would have been different if he had stayed in charge would actually have proved correct.

The expedition did leave room for some of the flaws in Ed's style to become apparent. Without his impetuousness he might have stopped after returning from low altitude and reacclimatised; and this would probably have prevented his altitude sickness.

Peter Mulgrew's own account of these events, *No Place for Men*, is a small, witty masterpiece of Himalayan mountaineering literature. It is also an interesting footnote to the literature of drug addiction. In terrible pain, he was prescribed pethidine, a highly addictive opiate. He tried to do without it but the pain in his feet was too great, and only the drug could ease it. 'Thus began the gradual infiltration of that insidious drug throughout my nervous system,' he wrote, 'accompanied by the relentless sapping of my willpower. In the months to come, my dependence on the drug became so great that I was unable to differentiate between pain and the need for pethidine.' Before long the nurse was having trouble finding a clear space to administer the two-hourly injections.

Hospital visitors did not include the British ambassador to Nepal, who at this time also served as New Zealand's diplomatic representative and might have been expected to call. Mulgrew noted that this personage went out of his way to avoid any contact with the expedition or its members. 'Maybe he had the well-bred Britisher's horror of wild colonial boys,' wondered Mulgrew. Or maybe he had the well-bred Britisher's horror of recalling the embarrassment of the 'race' to the South Pole.

Ed arranged, courtesy of the sponsors, for June Mulgrew to be flown up to be with her husband Peter while he was treated for his injuries. She did not know how badly hurt he was until she arrived, but she took the situation in her stride and set about doing what she could, including learning how to administer the two-hourly injections of pethidine under supervision.

June added to her medical mien by wearing a white shirt back to front, and was delighted when she heard herself referred to as the Memsahib Doctor. Her husband reported that her first shot practically 'pinned my arm to my chest'. She was accommodated in a guesthouse outside the window of Mulgrew's room, and he drew comfort from the fact that they could talk to each other from their beds on still nights.

It was decided to return Mulgrew to hospital in Auckland. Ed and June were on the flight with him; and the patient noted with some chagrin that his companions were treated to champagne that was forbidden to him. The *Auckland Star* was there to capture an incongruously jolly photo of the three of them sitting in the back of an ambulance on arrival.

Not long after his return, Mulgrew agreed to the amputation of both his legs below the knee. June was on hand when he woke from the operation; he then received a huge dose of morphine and lapsed into unconsciousness, gripping one of her fingers so tightly she could not free it, but had to wait until he awoke. Subsequently, pethidine would be the addictive painkiller administered. There followed a long recuperative period.

Ed gave Mulgrew a copy of *Reach for the Sky*, the biography of Douglas Bader, the former World War II air ace and double amputee. Mulgrew liked the gesture, though he didn't warm to the subject.

When the hospital told him it had been slowly reducing his dose of pethidine, he decided to go cold turkey. On hearing that decision the doctors sent him home, believing the more congenial surroundings would aid the process. He went through three days of terrible withdrawal symptoms and many more weeks of pain before finally learning to walk on artificial legs. He would go on to achieve success in business.

June showed remarkable courage and patience all through Peter's recovery. It would not be the last time her devotion would help a man back to normal life.

For Ed, the era of the great swashbuckling adventure was almost over. Instead, he was about to embark on a very different kind of adventure, one that he would regard as his greatest achievement.

CHAPTER 7
THE BEST ADVENTURE

Climbing a forbidding mountain and travelling halfway across a frozen wasteland are impressive achievements; but as Ed would have realised by now, they don't really change anything except the names in record books. They have no purpose. They are as much aesthetic activities as practical ones. Once you've been up a mountain, all that's left to do is go down again.

Building a school, however, changes lives.

Ed was brought up not just to do, but to do unto others as you would have them do unto you. Percy and Gertrude had planted the seeds of social conscience, and it was a big part of his character. 'A lot of it was a background of experience from my parents, who were very respectable,' Ed explained to the BBC in 1999. 'And my father in particular had strong feelings about Westerners supporting third-world countries. I suppose I absorbed this. When I became very friendly with the Sherpas and saw what they lacked—no schools and no medical facilities—I thought I should do something about it and I did.'

This is why he would always say the achievement of which he was proudest was the work he did with the Himalayan Trust. He would be directly involved from the time of its first project to his death, and the Trust itself continues to carry out an ambitious aid program to this day. It's not the wildest conjecture to believe that Percy would have been much more impressed by the work Ed did here than any number of mountains climbed.

The Trust took shape over a number of years. The first project was a school at Khumjung, an idea that had come up in a casual conversation around a fire with a group of locals. Ed asked if there was anything he could do for the people of the region.

'Burra sahib, our children have eyes but they are blind, therefore we request you to help with the school,' answered Sirdar Sherpa Urkien. Work on the school went on during much of the HSME, with Ed even managing to get funding for it from the expedition sponsor.

The fame that came from Everest was not an end in itself, but it could be a means to an end. Ed saw early on that it could open many doors. Everyone wanted to meet the Hero of Everest. And once he got in front of them, it seemed everyone wanted to give the hero money to help people in a remote, almost unknown part of the world. But Ed only pushed this up to a point.

Sarah Hillary suggests it may have contributed to the ease with which he shouldered the burden of fame. 'The fact is he had to be famous,' says Sarah. 'He had to have a profile to get the funding, so he realised that that was a necessary part.'

Peter Hillary, though, isn't convinced the fame was necessary. 'He did what he did because he wanted to do it,' says Peter. 'Everest gave him fame, but for him Everest moved right into the background fairly early on. You don't need to be Neil Armstrong or Ed Hillary to get a profile. [Success] comes down to your energy and drive. If he had been the second person to climb Everest, in which case no one would have known who he was, I am not sure he wouldn't have built the schools and hospitals, and I am not altogether sure he wouldn't have become famous for it.'

Peter credits Percy, as much as Everest, for the direction Ed's life took. 'Because of that family background—they were a deep, philosophical family, searching for things, for a good way of living, and I think the Himalayan Trust was his way of fulfilling that childhood experience. "What is the right way to live? Well I am going to build schools and hospitals in Nepal."'

Another man who segued from climbing mountains to changing lives—particularly those of young people, through the likes of the Sir Edmund Hillary Outdoor Pursuits Centre, which he launched in 1972—was Graeme Dingle; he believes Ed treated aid work like climbing a mountain.

'I am not sure you could say Ed was generous, actually,' says Dingle. 'It would be better to say he was a humanitarian and he was driven no matter what he did. So you go out to build a school for the Sherpas; you are not going to stop at the first road block you get to. You either go around it or you go through it.'

Ed himself told Mark Sainsbury that if he hadn't climbed Everest he would probably have spent his life as a beekeeper.

As with many other aspects of his life, when Ed was doing something that no one had done before, he made it up as he went along. That included learning how to capitalise on the value of his name. He was pushy on a mountain, and yet anything but pushy in other ways, as the folks at World Book Encyclopedia had noted.

'The thing that surprised me at the beginning was the lack of sophistication in the humanitarian stuff,' says Dingle. 'At one level there was huge intelligence, but you know with a name like [Hillary] you would go to a construction company and say, "Give us a module of a school." But he didn't do it like that. He would go and say to the Sherpas, "We will knock down a few houses, so we can get a supply of stones, cut down some forests so we can get some trees and we'll get roofing from New Zealand and carry it in." It didn't look particularly sophisticated but it was good because it got the Sherpas contributing equally.'

Dingle experienced the full force of Ed's reluctance to capitalise on his name—or let it be used in any context unless absolutely necessary—while he was helping the aid effort in the Solukhumbu. When the building of a hospital at Khunde was completed in 1966, Ed asked Dingle, who was a competent artist, to paint a sign for the front of the hospital. The eager young adventurer asked the hospital doctor what he should put on the sign.

'He said "The Hillary Khunde Hospital",' relates Dingle. 'So I had to make the board, plane it down and paint the sign—"Hillary Khunde Hospital". Then I went off to do a trek, and when I came back the sign had been torn down and this really rough thing left in its place. I was really pissed off, so I asked, "What's happened to my sign?" Ed had ripped it down because he didn't want his name associated with anything to do with the hospital. It was that modest side to him, and politically it was better for him that it wasn't up there. So there were murky things like that, that sort of disturbed him about me for years pretty much always throughout our relationship.'

Dingle had worshipped Ed as a young man, and became a lifetime friend after a rough start. 'I'd been selected to go to Antarctica and it was potentially a great exploratory journey,' says Dingle. 'There was no reason to choose me except I was really enthusiastic. Before the trip, I fell off a mountain and smashed myself up, but I still kept my place and went on the training week at Waiouru.

'I had with me one of the best Italian mountaineers, Carlo Mauri. He was incredibly sophisticated, confident and determined to get to Antarctica. One day we were milling about when suddenly Peter Mulgrew and Mike Gill and Ed Hillary appeared outside. [Ed was preparing to go on a different expedition.] Half of the guys just stood in awe of these three demigods.

'Carlo stuck his hands in the small of my back and said, "Go ask Sir Ed Hillary if I can go with him." This nineteen, twenty-year-old kid limping up to him with my smashed arm strapped to my chest. Ed was actually incredibly rude. He just went, "NO". It was absolutely brutal. I mean, I started off quite gently: "Ed, I want to introduce you to Carlo" and he said, "NO" and he looked absolutely blank. I thought, this guy is a really well-known mountaineer. Why wouldn't he know him? I told Ed he'd climbed a mountain with Walter Bonatti. When I mentioned Walter Bonatti, there was some recognition. I said, "He wants to come to Antarctica with you." He just went "NO". There was nothing else to talk about.

'I thought he was a rude prick at the time. I thought that was a huge disappointment. But when I started to become quite well known and was the first climber of all the European north faces in one season, Ed wrote to me and said, "Do you want to come to the Himalayas with me?"

'I said, "Yes, absolutely," so as soon as I met him I fell in love with him.'

From the start Ed was determined to give the Sherpas what they wanted—not what a Western philanthropist might decide they needed. At the same time, he wanted to make sure there was commonsense to it all, and that any initiatives would not do harm in the long term.

'He would never say, "Well if I was building this thing I would put a chimney on it," ' says Dingle. 'He would say, "How would you like it made?" They might say, "Well we don't like chimneys on buildings because that makes them cold," so Ed would say, "Let's make a building that's a compromise between what will work and what will work in your country."'

In the case of the school, for instance, he had tried to ensure that it would not become a factory turning out young people who no longer wanted to live in and contribute to their own area but would be seduced by the brighter lights of the big city.

'He didn't outright give money,' says Sarah. 'He would always expect something from the community as well, which seemed successful for the Himalayan Trust. If the community wanted it, they would have to provide the materials for the labour so it wasn't just handing over the money, which is a good concept and he actually did it with us as well, unfortunately.' Ed worked hard to ensure his own children didn't take money or possessions for granted: they had to work for something if they wanted it.

Much later he took a stand that was unpopular with many locals when he opposed the building of a luxury hotel that would have served as gateway accommodation to Everest. Ed was not against encouraging visitors as such, but this particular plan would have put an airport through Khumjung village, wiping out potato fields and houses. The locals were tempted by a generous offer and it took Ed no small effort to persuade them of the dangers the plan held in the long term. An alternative site was found.

Ed's decision to ensure that aid measures were Sherpa-led was reinforced by an abortive attempt to revolutionise local chicken-breeding practices. This incident is recounted by Mike Gill in his magnum opus about the Trust's work, *Himalayan Hospitals*. Ed procured New Zealand guidelines on poultry farming, which left the locals thoroughly bemused. In the end, it was neither poor farming practice nor unsuitable methods that brought the project to a halt, but a local weasel that reduced the flock to an unworkable number.

The projects undertaken by what became the Himalayan Trust were extraordinarily varied. A partial list appended to Alexa Johnston's biography of Ed includes schools, hospitals, airstrips, workshops, lecture rooms, bridges, water supplies and health clinics.

All Ed's legendary team-building skills came into play on these ventures. It needed a diverse group of talents to carry out such a wide range of projects. 'The great thing about Ed is that he recognised abilities in me that I didn't know I had,' says adventurer Murray Jones. 'In Nepal, it's not like you can run down to the hardware store and buy what you want when you want. Typically, we used No. 8 wire a hell of a lot for tying down buildings. That was the only thing we had available. So Rex [Hillary] and I were quite good at making do with what we had.'

'He put this extraordinary group of people together,' says Peter. 'There was this incredible sense of loyalty to him. I think people really loved the opportunities he gave them.'

'He would be very tolerant until the moment he needed them to do the job,' says Hilary Carlisle. 'He would expect them to do the job well, but he would get a bit impatient if they didn't.'

Such cases were rare, according to Tom Scott. 'People would say time and again, "He picked me out of the blue," and he would say, "You'll do," and they did. He had a very low failure rate.'

However, if the people he picked looked like they might not do, Ed had a temper that made itself felt. 'He was hard on himself and could be hard on other people in expeditions,' says Scott. 'Personalities have to work [on expeditions]. If you have one person causing problems, the whole thing is out of kilter.'

Ed resisted suggestions that his work was in any sense repaying a debt—the implication being that the Sherpa people had helped him get where he was and he owed them for it. 'It's much more a sense of friendship and admiration for many of my friends up here,' he told NZTV's interviewer Paul Holmes on his eponymous show in 1996.

Ed's approach to aid reflected many of New Zealand's most cherished national myths: it was practical yet imaginative; he found inventive solutions to many problems; and he achieved swiftly, where others might have intellectually over-engineered the thing to death before even starting.

One example of such a solution is quoted by John Hillary. 'There was a village where the women spent something like 80 to 85 per cent of their lives climbing up and down this hill to get water. So Ed put a quality pipe at the top and a tank at the bottom and ran the water down the pipe into the tank and completely and utterly, with two little tiny things, changed people's lives.'

John admired Ed for his hands-on approach to humanitarianism. 'There are a lot of people who do wonderful things but quite often they gather money and give it to the people. Ed didn't do that. He went to the people and said to them "What can I do for you?"'

Ed shared local control most conspicuously with one of his very best friends, Mingma Tsering, veteran of Makalu. 'I think his partnership with Mingma Tsering was one of the great things,' says Peter. 'The Sherpa man couldn't read or write, but he was a brilliant manager of people. I have seen so many examples where there would be industrial issues and he would sort them out just by going in and talking to people, cajoling them and saying "Let's go."'

Not everyone rushed to be part of Ed's humanitarian efforts, though. The Nepalese royal family certainly didn't. As Johnston describes, an invitation to a school opening in 1964 led to the first visit to the region by a member of the royal family. Ultimately, in 1972 an agreement was signed between the Himalayan Trust and the government of Nepal; but much of the painstaking work on that agreement was done by John Claydon—Ed's South Pole pilot and petrol procurer, now employed by the Asian Development Bank.

Ed wasn't always in gung-ho mode; he could be patient if there was no choice, and he waited for the Nepalese Government to get on side. And it's abundantly clear he couldn't have done it without Rex, who used to regularly be described as the unsung hero of the Himalayan Trust—though his contribution has been better acknowledged in recent years. When the *Holmes* show produced a segment on the Trust's work in 1991, Mark Sainsbury described Khumjung School as erected by 'the Hillary brothers'. Pat Booth became so exercised by the lack of recognition for Rex that he had hoped to nominate him for an award under the New Zealand honours system; but Rex died (in 2004) before that could happen.

Critics have accused Ed of keeping Rex out of the spotlight. The younger brother is depicted as the hands-on plodder, while Ed flew in and out collecting cash and finding things to do with it. John Hillary has a ready answer for that.

'Dad was still building schools and hospitals for Ed in Nepal when he was 75, so what does that tell you? He loved it. He built a lot of the schools and hospitals. Ed didn't really do the physical, actual hands-on building, but nobody would have worked there if it hadn't been for Ed. Dad went over 25 times, and you wouldn't do that if you didn't like your brother.'

'You take your family for granted, don't you?' asks Murray Jones. 'They are always there. Rex was incredibly loyal.' Peter Hillary says the only time Rex got annoyed was when the food was sub par.

Alexa Johnston describes an aura of unity around the three Hillary siblings that no outsider would have been able to penetrate.

The bond between the brothers and sister, who had clung to each other to counter what the outside world saw as the family's eccentricity, was stronger than any worries about who got the credit.

'He told me there was one photo of them on the roof line,' says Hilary Carlisle, 'and Uncle Ed's got the hammer and [Uncle Rex] said "It was the only time he picked up the hammer, and then he got the nail crooked."'

'Well that's true,' agrees Murray Jones. 'Ed was the organiser, and it took quite a lot of organising to get the materials to where you wanted. Everything had to be carried in—like the corrugated iron; the whole works. That was Ed's forte and Rex's forte was the building.'

We can only wonder how successful the Trust would have been if Rex had been in charge of the organising and Ed in charge of the building.

Norm Hardie, though he was critical of Ed's ventures on the Barun Valley and elsewhere, remained on the Himalayan Trust for 22 years. He says one of the reasons he eventually fell out with Ed was that the schools Rex was building weren't insulated properly.

'I bet you he never said it to my father's face,' responds John. 'Well, Dad isn't one for punching but I'd like him to show me one thing my father ever built that fell down. Did you ask [Hardie] if he could carry up the materials? The timber and tools, piping? Ask the Sherpas what they thought of their hospitals and schools. Don't forget these are probably the toughest people in the world and they have been living in those cold conditions all their lives.'

Ed expressed himself forcefully when he felt moved; but he also at times avoided confrontation and discussion, and it seems that any criticism of Rex—particularly by Norm Hardie—was ignored.

Any limelight that was shone on the Trust was inevitably directed at its figurehead; and credit did not always go where it was due. 'It was great with [Mike Gill's] *Himalayan Hospitals* book,' says Sarah, 'because so many people were finally recognised for their good work. Often everything was focused on Ed and that was a good way to fundraise, but there were all these good people working so hard and they were so passionate.'

These seem to have been Ed's happiest times. As Gill points out, the Trust work marked a time of inevitable change for Ed. 'He just loved being up there with Mingma Tsering and talking about doing things and making them happen. He loved planning things and he was really good at it. It was a wonderful thing for him, this transition from being an adventurer to being middle-aged, and realising it is getting harder and he has to keep doing famous things, so suddenly he has got this big new project which is open-ended and lasted him the rest of his life.'

At the end of the day there would be time for a beer and stories. Ed was a wonderful storyteller, but his ability as a raconteur has never quite been done justice in print or in any TV documentary. A Radio New Zealand *Spectrum* documentary (available online), recording a reunion of Trans-Antarctic Expedition members, reveals Ed in discursive mode among his peers, without the self-consciousness that often bedevilled his appearances on camera.

Even back home the work and its legacy were a point of pride for Ed. As Maggie Barry described it, 'he lit up when pointing out the framed picture on the living-room wall of a group of Nepalese children, now grandparents, who attended one of the schools he built there'.

If you were a family member or friend of Ed's, he would at least try and inveigle you into some involvement in the Trust's work. Many people ended up donating months, sometimes years of their own time, bringing their skills to bear in this environment.

Louise was also active on the Trust's behalf in Auckland. She brought rugs, crafts and other items back from Nepal and sold them to raise funds. She also gave talks to raise awareness.

Like their father, the Hillary children developed a social conscience early on in life, sparked by direct encounters with poverty. In *Keep Calm If You Can*, Louise described their concern about the plight of Tibetan refugees in Nepal. Ed was thrilled when the children set up a stall to raise funds by selling their toys. And in a peculiar foreshadowing of later events with the Trust, there was even a family feud over the use of the money they made; the girls gave it away without consultation, in Peter's absence.

'At first we found [Nepal] strange,' says Sarah, 'but we rapidly started liking it because of course our parents had made friendships, so the people were really kind to us. We were treated like family. We loved it because we went wild, we went feral really. We could run around the hills, we didn't have to wash very much. The Sherpa people are very warm, they like laughing a lot and they are very strong and active.'

'They were wonderful trips and wonderful family trips,' says Peter. 'It has been an incentive for me to try and do similar things with my own kids.'

Kevin Biggar is a good example of a young person who fell under Ed's spell and rose to the challenge. His high school raised funds for the Trust and sent students to Nepal to help on the projects there. 'In my year they sent four students,' says Biggar, who was one of the four. 'It was a big commitment—you had to take a whole year off school because the trip was three months of the academic year.'

As a teenager, Biggar had not hero-worshipped Ed. He hadn't played climbing Everest when he was little. When Ed spoke at his school, he was more interested in the afternoon tea than in the Famous Mountaineer.

By the time he got to the Himalayas, though, Biggar was in awe of the great man. This was the period when Ed was New Zealand's high commissioner in India; but in Nepal he was relaxed and entertaining, singing his trademark maudlin version of *There's a Bridle Hanging on the Wall*, and telling stories of Everest and the Pole.

Ed's standing with the local population only increased over the years. According to Louise, even in the early days she had trouble finding competent Sherpa babysitters because they were so in awe of her husband that they could only sit and stare at his children. Many—especially the early pupils at the schools the Trust established—described Ed as a second father. In the words of George Lowe, it was 'not too much to say many of the locals give him a godlike status'.

Miracles certainly seemed to follow the opening of the hospital in Kunde in 1966. Many in the region were afflicted with a disfiguring goitre, the result of iodine deficiency, and women with this condition risked giving birth to children with cretinism—severely stunted physical and mental growth. But regular injections of lipiodol remedied both the hypothyroidism and the resulting cretinism.

In later years Ed did the rounds of the region with a bag of Trust money in the form of US dollars—the universal currency—which he dispensed according to need. He held meetings where locals put their case for donations, and he judged them on their merits.

'I travelled with him and his bag of money,' says Tom Scott. 'People came and made petitions and bowed and scraped.' It was heady stuff. It occurred to Scott that if he were in Ed's position, it would take only fifteen minutes for him to turn into a not very nice person. 'He became a living god. He would give this largesse, that largesse, handing out money. He had all this power. Whether that is the best model for aid . . . At least not a penny was creamed off by the officials in Kathmandu.'

But there were some unforeseen consequences to Ed's approach. His wish that educated young people would stay in their communities did not come to pass. 'He knew he was altering something he loved,' says Scott, 'but it would be altered anyway, so he tried to alter it the way they wanted to.'

Lodges were built to cater for the growing number of Westerners wanting to attempt a climb or just visit Everest. As Scott notes: 'Sherpas, especially the ones who own the lodges, are some of the wealthiest people in Nepal. A lot are moving into Kathmandu, and why wouldn't you? It's a big city; the climate's more benign.' Other Sherpas were prospering too—such as those who were providing other tourist services and expedition support. Ed himself described the centre of his benevolence as having become the 'Remuera of Nepal', referring to the affluent Auckland suburb where he lived.

The area was becoming depleted, not just of people but also of trees. Deforestation was a problem, caused partly by the boom in tourism: timber was needed to heat water for travellers to bathe with. 'It almost takes a tree to give an American a shower,' says Scott. 'In a very short period of time they stripped the trail on either side of the walk into Tengboche.'

It may even be that the Trust played a part in the deforestation. Norm Hardie maintains that more timber was used than was necessary in the building projects—timber floors where concrete could have been used, for instance. Hardie berated Ed for accepting a Canadian forestry award under the circumstances. 'He said the award came with $10,000,' recalled Hardie.

Ed realised something needed to be done. 'He went to see forestry people in New Zealand,' says Tom Scott, 'and he asked:

What do we do? How do we go about it? The reforestation is such a long-term commitment. A tree there at four years old is only so high and would be much higher in New Zealand. It takes great patience. But they have done it.'

Three nurseries were established through the Himalayan Trust, and seedlings have been planted since 1984 with positive results.

The long-term commitment of the Himalayan Trust is one of its key characteristics. Not many benefactors stay involved—as Ed did—with one project for more than 50 years. However, not everyone involved in the Trust would share Ed's single-minded focus. The downside of such consistent commitment—and an unexpected one for the man once credited with being able to change his plan when it needed to change—was that he could not see alternative opportunities for aid. This would become a major dividing point in later years.

That was far in the future, though. In 1975, Ed, Louise and sixteen-year-old Belinda were planning to spend a year in Nepal: they would be based in Kathmandu and would build a hospital in Phaplu. Belinda would do her lessons with the New Zealand Correspondence School, and she and her mother intended to learn Nepali—something Ed was never able to do.

The Trust and its work had brought health, safety and education to the people of Solukhumbu. But to Ed's family and friends it brought discord and controversy—and the greatest personal tragedy of his life.

CHAPTER 8
THE CATASTROPHE

Even sitting here now as a 56-year-old man, in a way I still struggle to come to terms with that. Experiences like that are so shattering that I think you just have to learn to live with it. I don't think it's a case of ever really shedding the pain.
—Peter Hillary, on *Foreign Correspondent*

It was to be the beginning of a great adventure. Ed, along with Rex and others on the Himalayan Trust, was building the hospital in Phaplu. On 31 March 1975, Louise and Belinda were due to fly in from Kathmandu to visit Ed on site.

Louise was a notoriously nervous flyer, especially in small planes. Her description of one nerve-wracking take-off, in *Keep Calm If You Can*, has a haunting poignancy in retrospect: 'We taxied up the harbour and just as we were about a quarter of a mile from a bridge stretching across the water we started to take off towards it. I died a hundred deaths immediately and hated all pilots in general for not treating every passenger as a shaking nervous wreck. Of course we lifted smoothly and unhurriedly into the air.'

On this occasion, Ed stood waiting for his wife and daughter on the airstrip at Phaplu. He grew increasingly worried as time went by with no sign of the plane. When a helicopter hove into view in place of the single engine Pilatus he was expecting, he feared the worst.

The helicopter brought Elizabeth Hawley. A former *Time* reporter who had been based in Nepal since 1960, and who would go on to become a mainstay of Ed's Himalayan Trust, Hawley had been the first of the inner circle to receive the news that the plane carrying Louise and Belinda had crashed.

'Are they alive?' Ed asked her.

'I don't think so.'

'Shit, what will I tell the parents?' Louise's mother and father were in Nepal at the time.

The small plane had crashed on take-off, killing the pilot, Peter Shand, and all four passengers. The cause was a simple oversight: the locking pins that held the tail flaps in stall position had not been removed. Those on board never stood a chance.

Ed insisted on flying to Kathmandu and the crash site. 'Sometimes now I regret that I did this,' he says in *A View from the Top*. 'It was an awful sight to see my wife and daughter in this condition. For a number of years the picture I saw would come up in my mind with monotonous regularity. This helped make it difficult for me to recover from the experience.'

A photo of Ed at the site shows a man in pieces, seemingly drained of every vital essence. As Pat Booth described it: 'The grief is all over him.'

The bodies were cremated that night. 'It was a pretty terrifying sight, seeing the most important part of my life disappearing up into the cloud,' was how Ed described his reaction to the ceremony. 'Terrifying' was not a word he often used.

At the time his mother and sister were being cremated, Peter Hillary did not even know they were dead. He had been travelling in India and it was some time before he was tracked down and told the terrible news.

As for Jim and Phyl Rose, 'I think it was really hard on them,' says Sarah Hillary. 'They aged considerably.' Sarah had been in Auckland, staying at the family's beachside holiday home at Anawhata. Peter and June Mulgrew were in Nepal; they learnt the news on their arrival back in Auckland.

John Hillary was in Australia, and read about the accident in the newspaper. 'I didn't know who was in the aircraft,' says John. 'I knew my father was there so I was somewhat worried for a while till I found out he was okay. But it was pretty traumatic for him.'

Rex stayed as close as he could to Ed for the next couple of weeks; he was perhaps the only person close enough to be able to provide any support.

Peter Mulgrew flew back with Sarah, who was to get another shock when she arrived. 'I thought as soon as I saw my father everything would be all right, but when I got off the plane Liz Hawley was there and warned me he wasn't very good.'

He was terrible.

Ed had led a triumphant life up until then, and it had all been of his own making—he had always been in charge. Even the bad things that had occurred had been his responsibility and he acknowledged the errors he had made. But this was a game of the gods. This was his worst nightmare, and there was nothing he could have done about it. All his stamina and strength skills were of no use in the face of this cruel accident.

'We know what happened,' says Sarah. 'When we went there, we heard about what had happened to the plane from another pilot; we heard lots of other stories about it. But we didn't want to talk about it because it was so upsetting. We would all start crying—it wasn't just him.'

'We understood everything that happened,' adds Peter, 'including the pre-flight checks, what had happened in the aircraft, what Mum would have felt like.'

The same need that drove Ed to the crash site to view the wreckage for himself was presumably what led him to visit Peter Shand's father later. It was, according to Norm Hardie, a harrowing interview. 'Ed asked Jim Wilson and me to attend the meeting,' says Hardie. 'It is clear the locks had not been withdrawn and this made the plane uncontrollable in the air. The father struggled to try to blame the ground crew for not taking the necessary action. Ed expressed sympathy but it was very emotional for all four . . . On the way home, Ed said, "Of course, in the end it was pilot error."'

Ed's grief was bleak, deep and long-lasting.

'If we are talking about what his weakness was,' says Mike Gill, 'it was truly being unable to cope with what had happened with the deaths. There's not many people that would've been as shattered as Ed was. He absolutely loved Louise and Belinda. He didn't really handle the post-Louise thing well, but that's not a criticism; it is just built into his character, and how can you criticise him for that?'

Ed blamed himself for a long time, for reasons he explained to the BBC's *HARDtalk* in 1999: 'The main reason is that Louise hated flying in small aircraft—and she expressed this view quite often—but I always persuaded her to come on these flights on small aircraft in very rough country. Finally when the disaster occurred . . . I really felt that it was my fault. I felt that if I hadn't persisted in getting her to come to all these places and joining me, she would still be alive.'

It's an emotional, natural but irrational way of thinking; and Ed was eventually able to see that. 'Nowadays,' he continued, 'I've largely got over that feeling even though I sometimes still have an uneasy feeling about pushing her into doing things she didn't want to do.'

Guilt led to thoughts, obviously fleeting, of ending his own life. Ed wrote to his friends of these thoughts—as always, he was better able to express himself in letters than face to face. According to Peter, he wasn't the only one—'We all felt a little bit like that.'

Ed was able to break through the cloud of his own misery for long enough to see clearly the disastrous effect it would have on those who remained—his children, the Roses and his Himalayan aid work. 'I knew I couldn't wipe that all away by doing myself in.' Besides, as he said in another interview, 'I didn't know how to do it anyway, so the idea never developed into any strong feeling.'

So he carried on.

His first autobiography, *Nothing Venture, Nothing Win*, was due to be published around the time of the accident. 'Ed was meant to be going on this book launch tour, so he just decided to continue on with that,' says Sarah. 'We went on that with him and he met up with friends along the way who comforted him . . . but deep down there was this sadness where you just knew things weren't right and would not be for a long time.'

Eventually the three Hillarys arrived back in New Zealand. In the meantime Sarah had come to a conclusion: she would be the one to replace Louise and Belinda and would dedicate her life to helping Ed. But it soon became obvious that that wouldn't be possible.

Ed headed back to Nepal to carry on with his work: there was still a hospital to be built. Sarah went back too, to help Mike Gill with the film he was making about Ed. 'I went over as a sound person, because I was considering what I could do as a career. But it was in the days of very primitive sound. There was no digital anything and the recording device broke down. I remember being over in Nepal and thinking, I don't want to be over here anymore. It was too depressing.'

But the work was a balm for Ed. Years later Peter told ABC-TV's *Foreign Correspondent* program that Ed 'realised if he didn't carry on and complete Phaplu Hospital and some of the other projects it was just going to make it worse'.

All his friends wanted to help, but few of them were brave enough to try. On Ed's side, the emotional shutters went up; on his friends' side, this was Ed Hillary—if something was too much for their hero to deal with, what use could they be?

Graeme Dingle spent quite a bit of time with Ed over the next few years, but never in that time did Ed talk about his loss. 'The worst thing was—and I suspect many of his other friends were the same—we didn't know what to do. Had I been a bit older, I would have just got on a plane and been there for him. As far as I know, Peter Mulgrew was the only one who did that. I honestly did not know what to do. I don't handle death very well anyway.'

Ed, as we have seen, like most men of his time, was not emotionally expressive—or receptive. 'Even years later,' says Dingle, 'I wrote him a letter telling him what a great example he'd been to me and I went through that whole business of saying how at the time of Louise's death I just didn't know what to say to him. He never replied to it, so I don't know if he ever got the letter.'

'Dad received these things but he would never respond,' says Peter. 'It was just the way it was. He never responded to a lot of things. A lot of people wrote letters or would phone up and say things and he would just sit there. It wasn't a very good coping strategy, but that is what he did.'

Peter says that although he and his father talked about their loss, there were still 'some areas you just couldn't go to. I don't think anyone went there actually. He was this huge person—most people felt in awe of him. These friends were senior doctors, senior business people, leading climbers or just really good friends. And they didn't feel they could go there.'

Wally Romanes, who had taken part in the Makalu expedition, was obviously determined to do something, and came up with a touching solution. He 'would turn up [at Ed's house],' says Peter, 'mow the lawns and go. He was desperate to do something, but didn't quite know what to say. They didn't necessarily come in, but it was rather nice that people did these things for us.'

'We were going through quite a lot ourselves,' says Sarah.

'We'd lost our mother,' explains Peter. 'Everyone focuses on him and I understand that, but we were having our own struggles, that's for sure.'

Peter—like just about everyone else, it seems—had an image of his father as a man who was always on top of things; and he expected him to be the same now. But he realised, when he first saw Ed after the accident, that Ed was not sorting this out. 'It was the first time Ed wasn't in control,' adds Sarah.

Later, Peter and Ed would visit the airstrip at Phaplu, as if in hope that through some magic the plane with Louise and Belinda aboard would turn up after all. 'Dad and I would walk up and down, up and down. You just wanted to roll back time.'

Those around Ed felt for him; and they grieved for the loss of two such vibrant and loved personalities. Mingma Tsering had been devoted to Louise, and all three children were much loved by the Sherpas. And the grief endures. 'It is really painful and I don't want to talk about it to be honest,' says Murray Jones in 2012. 'Both the air accident and Ed's death is extremely painful still.'

When Tom Scott, interviewing George Lowe on camera at Ed's house in the 1990s, broached the subject of Louise and Belinda's deaths, the climber burst into tears and taping had to stop. 'That was one of the most devastating periods of my life,' said Lowe.

Rex Hillary's response was full of pathos, and an indicator of just what an effect Louise and Belinda had on those who knew them. 'Although I'd lost one of my own children and that was very painful,' said Ed's brother, 'I don't think any death affected me quite as much as the deaths of Belinda and Louise.'

In the midst of all this, Ed made the claim—for the first, but not the last time—that the accident had robbed him of the two people he loved most of all. Pat Booth heard him say it 'several times in my hearing'. It was repeated in the Academy of Achievement interview and as late as *View from the Summit*, which was published 24 years after the accident.

The statement made some wonder about Ed's feelings for the two children who were still alive; at best, he was being insensitive to their emotions. But it was not surprising, given Ed's nature. 'He had a ruthless honesty,' says Scott. 'If he behaved badly or was depressed, he said so. If he thought someone else had behaved badly, he said so. So when he said "two people most dear to me" that's what he believed. The publisher tried to get him to take it out. But it was the truth. He said it more than once.'

Ed had lost perspective. His tragedy was terrible, but not unique. He was not the first man to lose a wife and child in one awful moment. This calamity befalls people every day in motor accidents, fires and other forms of sudden death. Many of these people grieve and get on in a way that Ed could not bring himself to do.

'I think it shows the extent to which he'd turned in on himself,' says Gill. 'He couldn't see any loss except his. Peter and Sarah simply had to go their own ways, because suddenly there was no family left. It wasn't like the other half was being cohesive. Ed wasn't trying to hold that together either.'

'He stopped whistling,' says Peter. 'He never whistled again. He used to whistle and whistle . . . he would be so happy he would just whistle.'

In part, too, Ed's reaction was the single-minded reaction of the high achiever. If he was getting to the top of Everest, nothing else was happening. And if he was grief-struck, that was what his existence was about—there was no real room for anything else, even as he went through the motions of his regular activities.

Just as there was no one who could help Ed work through his sorrow, there was no one who could stand up to him and say, 'These words are hurtful. You are neglecting two people who are depending on you to support them. You have to stop saying this and help the two children you have left.' There was no one to remind Ed that he was still a father, and with that came responsibilities that did not disappear simply because he was in a bad way himself. It was his job to put Peter and Sarah's grief and recovery ahead of his own.

This was his most unheroic moment.

Eventually he came to understand what he had done. In *A View from the Top* he admitted, 'my sorrow and sadness about the whole activity affected me personally. I sometimes ignored the fact that my children were equally affected by this great disaster.'

When Sarah is asked about Louise and Belinda being the two people he loved most, she answers indirectly. 'I think in the beginning of the book he wrote, "You are the one that I really care about" to Louise and she was the focus—she was the top one. He loved his family and friends, but she was his support. It was a true deep love.' No one has ever doubted that.

So Peter and Sarah went their own ways.

Peter thinks that, in his case, the accident probably played a part in his decision to go into aviation and get his pilot's licence.

Sarah had been studying. 'After the accident happened I went back to Auckland but decided I couldn't continue my course, so I bummed around for a bit. But I did go back to varsity the following year, to Dunedin. It took a long time to sort myself out. I think I was quite self-destructive for a very long time. I was eighteen when they died, and by 21 I'd had a child, so I ended up having children very young. It got me into action once more because I realised I had to get a career as well, so I had to do that at the same time as having young children. So I think that pulled me together.'

Many people say there was a before Ed and an after Ed; that he never quite regained the spark he had when Louise and Belinda were still alive. But John Hillary maintains that Ed didn't change deep down—that his reaction was a normal one.

'For a long time he was really depressed about it and sad, which is hardly surprising,' says John. 'To lose two of your family members like that—and I know from personal experience—is very traumatic, especially if you loved them. But to say he changed dramatically, for me, is a load of rubbish. I never saw that in him. He did a lot of great things after they died. He carried on doing all the things he had been doing before they died and he carried very sad memories of them for a very long time.'

Asked after Ed's death whether he missed him, Mike Gill said, 'No, I wouldn't say I miss him [because] he was a changed person post-1975. He was much harder to get through to.'

Ed, whose unfeigned ebullience was a large part of his make-up, was also prone to, if not depression, at least the blues. Tom Scott notes that if you added up the number of times he referred to being 'a bit low' in print or interviews over the years 'you would say his resting condition is melancholia'.

He required the adrenaline of a challenge—whether of an adventurous or humanitarian nature—to get him motivated and keep him upbeat. So he would naturally have been predisposed to a strong reaction when faced with a trauma such as the death of Louise and Belinda. He also fell back on some traditional palliatives—alcohol and tranquillisers; he was consuming several scotches and sleeping pills every night. 'The combination of booze and drugs,' Ed says in *A View from the Top*, 'certainly helped me over that particular period.'

The months of grief turned into years, but eventually he started to come right. Ed refused to believe the adage that time would heal the wounds; but he did find that, ever so slowly, it helped them become less painful.

Former New Zealand Governor-General Dame Cath Tizard describes being present at one turning point. It was an era when friends' social lives consisted to a large extent of rotating Saturday night parties at each other's houses. She and her then husband Bob were family friends of Max and Lois Pearl's, who had spent time with Ed in the Himalayas and had been supporters of the work in Nepal.

'They rang and said they'd managed to persuade Ed to come around one night with just some close friends,' says Tizard. 'I didn't know then how depressed he had been after the deaths. We went around to the Pearls and Ed was very withdrawn and quiet. But they had got all his climbing mates up from the South Island. And late in the evening, when most of the guests had gone, someone brought up Gilbert & Sullivan and one of the chaps was a great aficionado. We started singing Gilbert & Sullivan, and Ed thought this was hilarious and perked up no end. Our singing was probably half drunken and terrible, but it was good fun. The Pearls told us later that for Ed that night was a turning point. The defining moment when he finally decided there was life after death.'

The recovery from the loss of Louise and Belinda had begun, but it would take another remarkable woman to complete the process.

CHAPTER 9
THE DHARMA BUMS

Ed was always happiest when he had an adventure to think about, and his lack of interest in such activities had been a sure sign of his depression. But in 1977 he was ready to get going again, albeit without the customary élan.

'During that time, after Louise's death,' says Graeme Dingle, 'the sort of contact [we had had], because I was living down the central North Island, was a bit harder because it was quite a trek to get to Auckland. Generally we could come when Ed told us to come, so he kind of closed down and didn't invite us to come up. But one day he called out of the blue and said, "Come up, we have some things to talk about." There was this fabulous gathering at his house and he said, "We are going to the Ganges."'

Although he could hardly be said to have recovered from his grief, Ed had found the energy and heart to start planning a great adventure. It was an idea that had come to him some years previously—a 2400-kilometre journey up the Ganges River to the Himalayas, with the last 160 kilometres on foot.

Ed always denied that he was in any sense a professional adventurer. 'I still regard adventure pretty much as a hobby, to tell you the honest truth,' he said in his Academy of Achievement interviews. 'And I think this approach to it keeps one refreshed almost. I think if you just regard adventure as a business, working becomes very boring as many other businesses can become. But even though adventure changed my life considerably, both in what I was doing and even economically, I've always regarded myself in a sense as a competent amateur. Because of that, I think a freshness has been brought to it, that every new adventure has been a new experience and great fun. I really like to enjoy my adventures. I get frightened to death on many, many occasions but, of course, fear can be, also, a stimulating factor. When you're afraid, the blood surges in the veins . . .'

In that statement we see that Ed had many qualities he shared with all great adventurers: a terror of boredom; a desire to doing something for the sheer love of it rather than the rewards; and a taste for fear and the resulting adrenaline. He was an amateur in the old sense—someone who did what he did for the love of it, and with little expectation of reward.

A 21st-century adventurer can, thanks to the far greater availability of media sponsorship opportunities, plan a calendar full of year-round escapades from one continent to another. But there was a trace of the Victorian gentleman adventurer in Ed, sallying off on a life-threatening jaunt whenever he came up with a good idea. And anticipation was half the fun.

'When he was planning the next expedition he would change,' says Hilary Carlisle. 'He could be sitting around not knowing what to do with himself and then he'd be planning something. He would have this board and he would be writing down things and rubbing them out. He just loved that.'

In some ways the jetboat journey from the Bay of Bengal up the Ganges and then to its source in the Himalayas was the most romantic and inspired of all Ed's adventures, albeit the least trumpeted. It combined the icy thrill of the mountains with the colourful landscape of India and its people; it connected Kiwi ingenuity with the spiritual element that could not be escaped when journeying past many of the most sacred sites in Hinduism. The Ganges is one of the most sacred waterways in the world, revered by those who depend on it for their very existence. And, as if to complete the picture, it ended unhappily for Ed, with the ultimate prize withheld from his grasp when it seemed just within reach.

And yet Ed was still the hard-nosed expedition organiser who chose to take the team he wanted—not the team who wanted to come. Among those who were keen to join the expedition was Peter Mulgrew. Despite his double amputation, Mulgrew had gone on to succeed in business and also to become a formidable competitor in ocean racing. He had been willing to follow Ed to the South Pole, come what may, and he had nearly died on Makalu; but Ed didn't think he was right for this trip and told his friend he wouldn't be going.

According to Alexa Johnston '[Mulgrew] was always quite a crusty or difficult man. I think Ed just thought, "This isn't going to work if he comes. It's a long trip and we can't afford to have it fall to bits." Also it was being filmed and you can't plaster over the cracks when things are falling to bits. That created a real rift.'

Those who did accompany Ed included his son Peter, then 23, and now-familiar names such as Mingma Tsering, Max Pearl, Murray Jones, Mike Gill and Graeme Dingle. Relatively new team members were Jon Hamilton—whose father, Bill Hamilton, had invented the jetboats that would make the expedition possible—and Jon's son Michael. Australian director Mike Dillon filmed the journey.

The plan was to take three boats as far as they could and then walk to the ancient holy city of Badrinath, before climbing one of the mountains whose peaks, Ed explained in *View from the Summit*, provided snow that melted and fed into the source of the Ganges.

One of the most important incidents on the trip came at Varanasi, the holy city where Hindus hope to end their lives because to die there is to go straight to paradise and be spared the rigours of more incarnations. It would be another turning point in Ed's recovery.

He related the incident for *HARDtalk*. 'Our trip on the Ganges was perhaps one of the most remarkable adventures we'd ever undertaken. Not only did we have the challenges and dangers of wild water and rock and so on, but we were also absorbed into the vast Hinduism of the river Ganges. All the priests in places like Varanasi welcomed us, blessed us, put dabs of paint on our foreheads and wished us well for the journey on. On one particular occasion—a very ceremonial occasion—this rather wild and furious young man got us to kneel down on the sand beside the river and then he pressed our heads onto the sand. Meanwhile little containers with little candles in them—he put them in the water and they floated away. It was a very emotional moment. I really at that moment felt a slight lifting perhaps of the sorrow that I'd experienced over the previous two or three years.'

Film footage of this incident bears out Ed's words to the detail. In the midst of a frenetic Indian scene, the young man's words cut through the cacophony and it is possible to see Ed, lost in meditative concentration, relax just slightly.

'The Indian people on that trip really were totally in awe of him,' says Alexa Johnston. 'There were literally millions of people— brightly coloured things, their turbans looked like hundreds-and-thousands. Everywhere they stopped, they got mobbed.' It being a river journey, Ed went with the flow. Johnston concludes: 'It made it easier, because he didn't have to resist what they were doing. He also said on that trip that they set off to have an adventure, but the people greeting them thought they were making a pilgrimage. By the end, Ed said, "We accepted it. We had a Hindu world view too."'

Ed was asked, 'These people think you're a Hindu god. How do you deal with that?' His answer was the only possible one—both accurate and irrefutable. 'I know I'm not, so it doesn't matter.'

'He never thought he was anything other than himself,' says Johnston, echoing the view of many others. 'That's hard to accept in today's world, where you can't believe that people who get such great accolades don't believe the myth. But he never believed the myth. That's something his difficult childhood gave him, I think.'

Of course, for those who had come along on the Ganges adventure and didn't experience deification, it wasn't necessarily easy to put up with seeing your mate being worshipped. Murray Jones admitted as much, while acknowledging he was seen as slightly divine by association.

'If I am honest,' says Jones, 'I didn't behave particularly well. I had great difficulty accepting the adulation the Indian people were giving us. It was like being a rugby star in New Zealand, and sometimes you deserve it and sometimes you damn well don't. Because we were going on this trip that Ed was organising, the Indian community came out in throngs. Ed caught the Indian imagination, because we were doing something that they regarded as reasonably sacred. You don't just come down to the Ganges at the drop of a hat, and that caught their imagination.'

Compared to the vicissitudes of Everest, the challenges of the South Pole and the terrors of Makalu, this adventure seems like a spree, an early form of adventure tourism for some not-so-young people letting off steam. 'We had fun on those jetboats and seeing those tigers in the wild was fascinating,' says Jones.

Eventually a waterfall put an end to the boats' progress. After reaching Badrinath there was still a mountain to climb. A base camp was set up at 4570 metres. Ed made it as far as a camp at 5480 metres before he began to feel unwell; he was suffering from altitude sickness yet again.

'He developed an issue with altitude that got worse and worse,' says Peter. 'I mean, when Dad had collapsed it was only a couple of years after Mum had died and I thought I was going to lose my father as well. Fortunately, with altitude sickness, if you get to people quickly enough and you get them down, it is a quick solution.'

Altitude sickness is 'fluid flowing into your brain and lungs', explains Peter. 'It is suffocating. If it was pulmonary oedema, which is what he had, there is pink foam and you are suffocating; you need to sit up so the fluid is at the bottom of the lung. If you lie down it is across the whole lung, which is worse. But if your lung fills up— it's all over. He hadn't got that bad, but he wasn't that good. But we got him down and he very quickly started to recover.'

Some of his companions thought he was dead or near dead, but he regained consciousness as he was being carried to a lower altitude. They didn't bother putting him on a stretcher or trying to wake him. They dragged his whole tent—complete with the sleeping bag containing Ed—downhill.

Murray Jones accompanied Ed to Badrinath and safety, while the others continued their ascent to the top of Akash Parbat, where they sprinkled water that had been taken from Mother Ganges at the start of their visit, completing a magnificent, mystical circle of life.

It was a disappointing end to a magnificent escapade. Yet again, Ed had overexerted himself and was lucky to be alive. It was as if, as a young man, he had used up so much of his physical resources, his stamina and his all-round superhuman abilities, stretching his body to unimaginable limits, that he was now burning out at the relatively early age of 58.

In the years to come he would have more life-threatening incidents, simply because avoiding high altitudes would have meant staying away from his beloved Solukhumbu and his work for the Himalayan Trust.

India and Nepal rekindled such spiritual inclinations as Ed had. He denied that he was a religious person but he had, as we have seen, a thoughtful, philosophical disposition. The youthful involvement with Radiant Living had been a dead end, but there were plenty of other paths to explore, and it was the religions of the East that he found most congenial. 'I have no particular religious beliefs at all,' he told the Academy of Achievement, 'but I am interested in all religions. In Tibetan Buddhism, one of the strongest features is that they believe that everyone must choose their own path in life.'

Ed was always enormously respectful of other people's views. 'He worked very hard to help Sherpas rebuild monasteries,' notes Tom Scott. 'When the monastery at Tengboche burnt, he and [climber Reinhold] Messner led a worldwide campaign to rebuild it. I have been to the opening of three or four monasteries with Ed. He thought Sherpas should keep their culture alive as long as possible.'

Ed would go into battle to protect one religion from another, even when he adhered to neither. Tom Scott tells a story of a group of Buddhist boys from Nepal: 'Some young guys went to Kathmandu on scholarships. They rang up very distressed, saying the priests were putting pressure on them to convert from Buddhism. Ed was furious. He got on the phone and within 48 hours these kids were shifted to another school, where they could retain their faith.'

For himself, Ed trusted in Ed, not God: 'I've always had the feeling that, if you're in a difficult or dangerous situation, doing a little praying, probably you're chickening out on the deal. It's up to you to make the decisions and carry on if you want to reach the top.'

It's a hard man who sees praying as a sign of weakness. At one time, though, there were as many atheists up mountains as there were in foxholes. 'I'll always remember one little incident,' he told the *Listener*, 'I was climbing in the Southern Alps and I was climbing out along a long narrow ridge, and it was quite difficult for me in those days, and quite challenging. You know I was never a very religiously inclined person, but I was sufficiently fearful on this occasion to maybe say a little prayer or two. I would say this little prayer and after I'd gone a little further along the ridge I said to myself, "What are you up to? You got yourself into this problem, you're the one who has to get yourself out of it." And I surely did. So I refused to be dictated to by any source really, if there was any possible way of me doing it myself.'

So Ed's attempt at prayer confirmed his belief in its lack of efficacy and the need to rely on one's own resources. When, in his writings, Ed questioned the capitalist system, for instance, his thinking is based on his own close observation and experience— in this case, of the crass consumerism of early 1960s America, which appalled him. In a few years a whole counterculture would be echoing his thinking.

Many of his qualities—egalitarianism, religious tolerance— are the ones New Zealand would have used to describe itself before the 1980s exalted free-market survivalism to orthodoxy. Near the end of his life, Ed was increasingly out of step with his country philosophically; but he was too big a figure for anyone to point this out to him. 'I am not one of those people who

Ed and Louise leave the chapel after their 1953 wedding. George Lowe (left) was the best man. (Courtesy APN)

Ed (center) and George Dufek (left) meet Vivian Fuchs (right) at the South Pole in 1958. (Courtesy Alexander Turnbull Library)

On return from the South Pole, Ed became the public man again when giving this speech in 1958. (Courtesy Alexander Turnbull Library)

The great friends, Ed and Tenzing Norgay, meet in Wellington in 1971. (Courtesy Alexander Turnbull Library)

Ed (second left) with Queen Elizabeth II and other members of the Order of New Zealand in 1990. (Courtesy Alexander Turnbull Library)

The hero returns. In 2003 Ed celebrated the fiftieth anniversary of his and Tenzing Norgay's Everest climb with a street march through Kathmandu.(Courtesy APN/Paul Estcourt)

Ed received an Honorary Doctorate from the University of Waikato with June by his side in 2006. (Courtesy APN/Sarah Ivey)

Sarah and Peter Hillary at Middlemore Hospital where a ward was named after their father in 2010. (Courtesy APN/Greg Bowker)

believe . . . that every American could . . . become President of the United States,' he said once. '. . . But, I do think that virtually everybody that's born has the ability to be very competent at doing something. It's far more important to set your sights high. Aim for something high, and even fail on it if necessary. To me, that's always been more impressive than someone who doesn't ask for very much and achieves it.'

The New Zealand public didn't always agree with his attitudes. Perhaps they tuned out his comments on religion in order to be able to keep him as their hero. Or perhaps they saw his willingness to say what he really thought—even when it might be unpopular— as another kind of heroism.

It's hard to know why people kept asking Ed about him being a hero given the number of times he had denied that description. Probably Achilles was the last hero who actually owned up to being one. Yet Ed often described himself in ways that made clear his heroic attributes. It's heroic, for instance, to feel the fear and climb the mountain anyway.

Ed enjoyed a 'sense of challenge', and that was what kept him going, he said on *HARDtalk*. 'I was scared stiff many many times. Being afraid would often force me to take actions which normally I would have regarded as unwise or impossible. Instead I would charge on and carry through the problem and hopefully get to the destination. I believe that being able to do something first in the world is one of the most satisfying experiences that you can ever have.'

He elaborated on this to the Academy of Achievement: 'There's simply no question that, if you're doing something that has the possibility that you may make a mistake or something may go wrong and you'll come to a rather sticky end, this, I think, does add something to the whole challenge. You really feel you're doing something exciting and perhaps a little desperate, and, if you're successful, it certainly gives you that little bit more satisfaction.'

Tom Scott, though, is sceptical of Ed's refusal to accept the hero label. He was present when Ed unveiled a statue to Tenzing Norgay and made a speech in which he claimed that, though he did not regard himself as much of a hero, Tenzing undoubtedly was one.

Given that their achievements were essentially equivalent, and that Ed by most accounts went on to achieve more than his climbing partner, it's hard to see how one could be considered a hero and the other not.

But Ed had an answer for that. He told the *Listener* that he thought his assessment of himself and the Sherpa 'was true. I came from New Zealand and I worked hard, but lived in a comfortable environment and I didn't really want for anything, like most New Zealanders. But here was Tenzing, who really had nothing but a very strong desire to climb Everest, and I respected his determination to do his best on the mountain. I admired him for that.'

As for statues of himself, he was not happy when a bust was mounted as a tribute at the school in Khumjung. In fact, he never saw it. Tom Scott saw it on a visit to film a tribute to Ed. 'We are very pleased with the statue of the burra sahib,' his guide told him.

'I don't think the burra sahib would be very happy,' said Scott.

'The statue is not for the burra sahib. The statue is for us.'

In a way, this is a metaphor for the way Ed's own country viewed him. As will be explained later, New Zealanders needed a great man, and he was it. Their feeling was: 'He's our great man and we are very happy with him.'

'Although Ed was ambitious and had an ego and knew exactly what he had done and the scale of it, he kept it in proportion,' says Scott.

Ed understood that he was, in a sense, a fictional character. 'The media created a hero of Ed Hillary,' he said in *A View from the Top*, 'whereas I know very well I'm a person of modest abilities. But I do take a little bit of credit for taking advantage of opportunities that arose . . . Although I don't always follow the rules, I've had the good fortune to be ultimately successful.'

Everyone who knew Ed says there was no difference between the public and the private man. Yet Ed himself said frequently that he had to struggle to keep the two apart: 'The main thing was that, as long as I didn't believe all this rubbish that was written, I would be okay. I never did believe it. And I think I've survived reasonably well. I never deny the fact that I think I did pretty well on Everest. On the other hand, never for a moment have I ever suggested that I was the heroic figure that the media and the public were making me out to be. The public really like heroic figures that they can look on with great admiration, and whether it's true or not doesn't seem terribly important.'

CHAPTER 10
ANOTHER CHANCE

Ed needed rescuing. Not from the bottom of a crevasse, the middle of a frozen waste or the top of a mountain—but from his deep pit of black despair. There had been encouraging signs that he was finally going to get over the loss of his wife and youngest daughter, but he couldn't quite seem to cross the line. It was his good friend Peter Mulgrew's widow, June, who would come to the rescue.

Peter Mulgrew and Ed had ceased to be close in the years since Makalu. There were several points of contention: one was Mulgrew's disappointment at being passed over for the Ganges trip; another was disagreement over the affairs of the Himalayan Trust. Disagreement over the Himalayan Trust would become an increasing feature of Hillary family affairs over the years.

Mulgrew's career had flourished—he had become general manager of industrial manufacturer Alex Harvey Industries, and a director of commercial giants such as AHI Aluminium and Comalco.

According to Norm Hardie, who was also on the Trust, Mulgrew's increasingly sharp commercial acumen, as he ascended the business ladder, led him to push for a more business-like management structure and record-keeping for the organisation. Ed, on the other hand, seems to have functioned on an ad hoc basis with the Trust, doing what was necessary to get the results he wanted and shunning what didn't seem so important. It was what happened in Nepal that mattered, not what was kept in filing cabinets in Auckland. Mulgrew, possibly frustrated at Ed's continuing inability to yield supremacy in any area where he faced competition, ultimately resigned from the board of the Trust.

Sarah Hillary contends that the falling out with Mulgrew began after Louise and Belinda died. 'I think it had something to do with paying for my airfare. There was a bit of a fight about that. I think it was that Peter had taken me to Nepal. For Ed this was really a terrible time and you can overreact. I think they had been really close friends until that point. They were both quite driven people and they both took offence. Ed wanted to pay him back, but he didn't want Ed to pay him back.'

Despite their personal differences, Mulgrew and Ed were taken on by Air New Zealand as guides when it began operating scenic flights to the Antarctic because they had both spent time on the frozen continent. The hero of the Race to the Pole and his doughty mate were perfect for the job, and they took turns going on the trips. Ed was down to be on Flight 901 on 29 November 1979 but had to reschedule. Mulgrew went in his place and was among the 257 passengers and crew who were killed instantly when their DC10 crashed into the side of Mt Erebus.

Although June and Peter had drifted apart over time and were separated at the time of the crash, it was the most bleakly ironic of tragedies. Louise and Ed and Peter and June had been close friends for many years, sharing good times as a foursome, travelling in Nepal together and enjoying each other's company back in

Auckland. And now, two of the four had died in plane crashes that had a strong connection with Ed's activities.

It was natural—if misguided—for people to wonder if Ed felt some sort of guilt, given that his old friend had taken his place. Here he was, just dragging himself out of his depression and visited by another calamity.

But the adventurer knew that chance holds all the cards in such cases. 'I don't think it would have remotely resembled the blame he would have laid on himself about Louise,' says Mike Gill.

Ed and June grew closer and eventually would marry.

Inevitably Louise and June—both twelve years younger than Ed—would be compared. For some, their very friendship was an unlikely pairing.

June's forceful personality made a big impression on everyone who met her. She may have been the epitome of 1950s suburban domesticity in the early years of her marriage to Peter Mulgrew, but she showed enormous strength in nursing him through the twin traumas of amputation and drug addiction.

Mike Gill describes Peter as 'a hugely determined and tough man' who could not be said to be 'second to June'. He describes their relationship as being like 'two rocks hitting against each other'. Gill remembers June in the early days as 'a more compliant, more womanly sort of person, but she had a hard life'.

Ed's first wife had been courted by a slightly awkward adventurer on the way up. His second wife, June, would marry a man who was not only the country's most respected citizen, but a world figure. She would need to be a strong personality in her own right for them to have anything like an equal relationship. Fortunately, June also shared Ed's enthusiasm for things Nepalese. Twice a year, beginning in 1975, she led trekking parties to Nepal as well as to Kashmir—an activity that requires initiative and resourcefulness.

Many observers describe June as a woman with a line-in-the-sand approach—a powerful person in her own right, very determined, strong-willed. 'June is totally different from Aunt Louise,' says Hilary Carlisle. 'Aunt Louise came from the heart—she was heart based. I am not sure June is heart based; she is more head based. Louise would do things like include the family. [. . .] She and Ed were young adventurers together—it was an adventure love story. With June, the adventures were over, but it was actually maintaining and servicing the requirements of the adventurer.'

'She can be very witty,' says Sarah. 'She is very funny; but the problem is she is very definite about things.'

Peter, whose relationship with June would grow increasingly fraught, describes her as 'very black and white'. And according to Tom Scott, 'June is really intelligent and a lot of fun, but she can get things wrong and be difficult.'

Climber and Trust member Murray Jones liked both Louise and June, but acknowledged their vastly different personalities. 'If [June] wanted something, she used to go for it in a very determined way. I have argued with her strenuously on many occasions. I have crossed her more than anyone else in this bloody world . . . She never approved of the way I dressed, because I am a real country boy. I am a Southern man who wears shorts everywhere and that's not the done thing in Remuera.'

Exactly when Ed and June might have developed the sort of friendship that can grow into a relationship and marriage is not clear, although it's worth noting that June reminded the *New Zealand Woman's Weekly* in 1985 that the magazine had been chasing the story for 'about eight years'. With the trekking, June was 'in Nepal once a year and then Kashmir in their summer, and so when Ed was in the Himalayas—because he'd go for six to eight weeks at a time—I'd see him and so it just wound up, I suppose'.

A man in his late fifties seeking a wife looks for different qualities in a partner than a man in his thirties does. Before there could be any sort of relationship, Ed had to be in a fit state to have one, and June's first job was to help him rekindle the joie de vivre that had always been a large part of his character—flipside to the melancholic tendencies—and that he still hadn't quite regained.

Hilary Carlisle, who describes June as focused and driven, says: 'She chivvied Ed out of the darkness, which took quite a bit of effort and time. He wasn't well. She provided him an infrastructure that enabled him to be out there in the public and raise money and keep work going for the Himalayan Trust and all the other things. He wouldn't have been able to do it for so long without her. She was also younger than Ed, so she had a bit more energy. She was quite tenacious and she was the one that would jolly him along and say "Come on Ed let's go for a walk."'

'He was never easy going, so she certainly helped him out of it,' says Mike Gill, who notes that June was a great support to Ed in his work as well as at home. 'He needed a companion ... He needed the emotional support, because Ed could do the organising himself but you can't buy the emotional support.'

'Ed would not have lived as long if it had not been for June,' says Murray Jones. 'June was always beside Ed, managing his affairs. The children weren't.'

This might be a strange comment to make about the dynamic between parent and child. People in their sixties don't expect to depend on their children, and adult children don't expect to have to provide the sort of emotional support for a middle-aged parent that a husband or wife would.

Yet so many people put themselves out for Ed—inspired by his example or the desire to be near him, or because he exhorted them to do more than they thought possible—that the expectation arose that his children would do the same. And those who have that expectation make Ed's mistake: he failed to note that Peter and Sarah were devastated by the loss of two people they loved, too.

Whatever else may have been missing in their lives, Peter, Sarah and June weren't short of people with opinions about how those lives should be conducted. The one person who could and should have expressed an opinion—Ed—appears not to have done so.

June had her work cut out getting Ed back in shape—but she had done it before. 'He was on heavy medication and she managed to wean him off that,' says Murray Jones. 'She managed him. While she was quite pushy, she made sure he got plenty of exercise and ate good food.'

'It was certainly great she was there,' says Sarah, 'because I think Ed really needed to be in a relationship. He'd been married for so long and he felt tremendously lonely, so the house was like a museum. Everything was exactly where it had been. [There was] a friend who did the cleaning and every time we tried to move anything, she would move it back to exactly how it had been. It couldn't go on forever like that.'

The one person who doesn't believe June was the crucial factor in Ed's return to normal functioning is Peter. 'I don't think June brought him out of depression,' he says. 'I just think it took him fifteen years to climb out of depression. But he needed company . . . He needed to have a woman there, but I think it was a long hard road. I think the whole psychological business had to run its course and it was a very long, deep business for him.'

Ed, who was not comfortable talking to any great extent about his feelings except in letters to one or two people—notably Louise when she was alive—described the burgeoning relationship with characteristic brevity in his writing.

It's often observed that having children is the hardest job most people will do in their lives. And for those who have had to parent other people's children it can be even harder. The role of stepmother is a difficult one to fill, especially for a woman who is called upon to take the place of a much-loved mother. Some step-parents are accepted from the start. Some take a pace back and let a relationship evolve. Some never get a chance.

As stepmothers go, the odds should have been in June's favour. She didn't come with a lot of the problems that are often present to sour the relationship. She was certainly no gold-digger in search of an income rather than a companion. Peter and Sarah were both in their mid twenties, so they didn't need a new mum. And June already had two children—her daughters Robyn and Susan; she didn't need a new family.

A big problem for June, as far as fitting into the Hillary family went, was that she wasn't Louise. 'She said several times,' says Tom Scott, '"I get older every year—bits fall off. Louise is forever 44." Louise got more and more sainted with every passing year.'

Ed and June didn't have the sort of blended family where the kids need to get on because they have to share rooms and there are fights over whether or not everyone goes to the same school. But it still had the potential to be a real family, if the work was put in and the will was there.

However, tension and personality clashes, particularly between Peter and June, seem to have been part of the dynamic from the start. Peter is a man who feels things keenly. His stepmother keeps her own counsel. 'June is closed and really unwilling to open herself up,' says Mike Gill, who eventually fell out with her. 'You just have to look from a distance and peer through cracks in the door.'

Hilary Carlisle tried to keep a balance between the sides in what she says was a difficult relationship from the start. Her position was probably easier because '[June] wasn't my stepmother. I made it my business to get on with everyone and that's my role in the family and I try to maintain it.'

'I think she felt when she got married to Ed she didn't necessarily want to like his friends,' says Sarah. 'But I guess that's what happens when people get together—it's a different dynamic. I wouldn't say she disliked all of them, but there is a new dynamic going on; there are the complicated family relationships. It's a tricky situation, so many things [have] changed.'

Having initially resisted any suggestions they should marry before Ed took up his post as high commissioner in India, the pair did in fact wed in 1989. The ceremony was performed by an old friend, Auckland mayor and later governor-general Cath Tizard. 'When she heard that I had said I was marrying Ed Hillary,' Cath Tizard says, laughing, 'June said, "I think I might be present too."' The joke has become part of both the Tizard and Hillary families' folklore.

Ed told Peter by letter of his wedding plans.

The ceremony was an informal affair at the Remuera Road home. Sarah describes it as a great celebration. Years later, both Sarah and Peter would note the contrast between this relatively relaxed event and the pomp and ceremony of Ed's state funeral.

'The wedding was funny,' says Cath Tizard. 'I think it was her family that said they ought to get married. I remember Ed saying, "I don't know what we're going through all this for. I thought we were perfectly all right the way we were," and the family shouting him down: "Be quiet. Calm down." He wasn't upset; but if it had been up to him, it wouldn't have happened.'

Ed came to rely increasingly on June and she proved to be eminently reliable—a doting and devoted support in all sorts of ways. 'In the space of about a year she decided to change his wardrobe,' says Tom Scott. 'Ed went from wearing old man's clothing to wearing Rodd & Gunn-type sweatshirts. She sharpened him up. And she got his hair right. It was just starting to thin and recede, so she carefully plastered it. She made certain he shaved and the nasal hairs were attended to. Ed was just a mess, not looking after himself for the two years of grief.'

'I always got the impression they were comfortable together and she was doing the right thing,' says Pat Booth. 'I couldn't imagine Ed getting away with anything she disagreed with, without her telling him she disagreed.'

'The age difference thing was very big,' comments Mike Gill. 'At 80 a lot of energy is drained away.'

'He lost his hearing aid once when we were [in Nepal],' says Tom Scott, 'and June gave him bollocks. "They're very expensive those hearing aids, Ed, very expensive." "Sorry, June, it must be here somewhere." And we turned the room upside down looking for it.'

'He loved someone caring for him,' says Murray Jones. 'He didn't want to end up in an old people's home. He said about Louise, he married a younger woman because she could look after him when he was older. But that's not the real reason—the reason is he loved her.'

Reporter Mark Sainsbury, filming a story on Ed in Nepal for the *Holmes* show, noted that he could look grumpy on occasion. 'We also realised how important June Hillary was,' says Sainsbury. 'Once there was a school we were supposed to go to. "I'm tired," said Ed. "No, Ed, you've got to go," June said. She knew people had been sitting out in the sun waiting for him. He probably would have gone anyway, but she was good at keeping him on track.'

Ed himself described June as a very strong influence, 'and particularly now in my ancient years there is no doubt at all: if there's a decision to be made, quite often June is the one who makes it.'

CHAPTER 11
LIKE FATHER, LIKE SON

If Peter Hillary were anyone else's son, he would almost certainly be regarded as one of the world's great adventurers. Firsts include the first ski descent of Mt Aspiring; and the first high-altitude traverse of the Himalayas—a 50,000-kilometre trek from Kanchenjunga to K2, with Graeme Dingle. He has climbed the seven summits—the highest peaks on each continent—including Everest twice, in 1990 and 2002. He came close to death on K2; and survived a hellish journey on foot to the South Pole.

Charismatic and passionate, he is a compelling speaker and an engaging writer with six books to his credit. He has a pilot's licence and, in his mid fifties, still acts as a mountaineering guide from time to time on peaks as challenging as Mt Cook. And he is a mainstay of the Himalayan Trust, continuing Ed's work in Nepal.

And yet ... there hovers about Peter the impression that he has spent his life trying, and failing, to measure up to his giant of a father. And no matter what Peter did, Ed appeared to remain unimpressed. The father was always polite in acknowledging his son's achievements—just not very enthusiastic.

There was a rare nod of approval for the record late in Ed's life, when Peter made his second summit of Everest. 'I think I felt more excited at that moment, and Peter felt more excited,' Ed told the *New Zealand Herald*, 'than I did when we made the first ascent of Everest nearly 50 years before. Peter climbed it for the second time. I've only done it once, I'm sorry to say. It was a good moment to have one's son doing even better than I had before.' Ed was 82 then and such effusive public praise—'a good moment'—had been a long time coming.

Peter grew up both proud of his father's fame and burdened by the legacy. The youth he describes in *Two Generations*, the book of which he and his father each wrote half, was a serious child, not a loner but lonely; not given to boisterous social activities; and unfulfilled by the usual adolescent distractions. This boy grew into a stroppy adolescent who, like many intelligent teenagers, had little tolerance for school subjects that did not interest him—giving him a reputation as an adequate but not exceptional student.

There is much in Peter's description of himself that could equally apply to the young Ed—solitary and thoughtful. One notable difference is that Ed, unlike his son, was an enthusiastic participant in team sport.

His father expected Peter to be self-reliant from an early age, although he was sometimes thwarted by Sherpas. Once, camping in Nepal, Peter was with his sisters in a tent that collapsed when Belinda tripped over a pole. Ed yelled to eleven-year-old Peter to get up and fix it. Before he could do so, Mingma Tsering had seen to it.

But Ed was not careless of Peter's personal safety, as one might expect of someone given to high-risk pursuits himself. When their son wanted to get a motorcycle on which to travel to university, Ed and Louise were reluctant; but eventually they agreed to allow him to have one, as long as it was no more than 90cc—and they bought it for him.

Not long afterwards, Peter persuaded Louise to act as guarantor for the purchase of a 750cc bike, without Ed's knowledge. When Ed found out, he was furious and he and his son did not speak to each other for a fortnight. Ed chose not to relate this incident in either of his autobiographies.

Much of the Hillary children's early years was spent travelling, following their questing father in his relentless flight from boredom. Peter was ten when Ed took him on his first climb—up Mt Fog in the South Island with Mingma Tsering, who was on holiday in New Zealand. He was roped between the two older men and, struggling to match their pace, slipped more than once, sliding downhill until the rope stretched taut and halted his progress so he could be reeled in. He was never afraid.

'I thought there was Ed Hillary, this is my father, this is Mingma—what could go wrong?' says Peter. 'So if I am rocketing down a slope, a young kid, I thought everything was fine because *boing!*—up you come. They fulfilled all of my faith in them. I just felt that this was Dad's show, whatever we were doing, and he would sort things out and he always seemed to.'

Most boys—at ten at least—think their father is Superman. Peter's father actually was Superman—although he would later find out that his father was not invulnerable, after all.

'One of the reasons why I was so shocked when my mother and sister were killed, when I saw Dad . . . even with this terrible thing that had happened and I was so heartbroken over . . . you thought he would sort it out, because he sorts everything else out.'

If Ed was hard on Peter, 'Peter was a strong-willed person, too,' says Mike Gill. 'He could be angry and difficult. He certainly wasn't an easy teenager. He just didn't like going to school, and there was nothing obvious he could drop into. Some people are lucky that, quite early in life, they find something that absolutely possesses them and they can follow it through and they are happy with it. But Peter seemed condemned to copy Ed.'

The tale of Peter's youth most frequently told, perhaps because it epitomises the complications that come with having a famous parent, is his practice of using an alias when he took holiday jobs, calling himself Peter Hill. It got him out of having to answer the questions that would inevitably come if he was identified as Ed's son.

Peter shared some adventures with his father, too. In 1979, he was a member of the Ocean to the Sky Ganges expedition; and he later accompanied him to the North Pole, meaning that both men had achieved the rare hat-trick of standing on both poles and atop the world's highest peak.

Ed described Peter on the Ganges trip struggling with the role of famous son. A constant on the journey was the number of people wanting to greet the living god wherever they went. And if he wasn't available, the son of the living god was the next best thing. For a young man with a self-conscious streak, this was punishing. When the cameramen pointed Ed out to some locals wanting autographs, Peter exploded, and Ed—no stranger to bouts of bad temper himself—had to try to talk him down.

'I can remember a couple of times when I was a bit fiery and I felt we really needed to push on and go for whatever it was,' says Peter of travelling with his father. 'I wasn't the only one, either, because a lot of the younger members—Murray Jones, Graeme Dingle—were all in the same boat. They were young then, impulsive—so that just comes with the territory.'

'In many ways Peter is a chip off the old block,' says fellow adventurer Dingle, who has had many encounters with Peter over the years. 'I think, when you get two similar characters, you are going to have some tensions. You have a young male and an older male. When we were making the *Kaipo Wall* film [for *The Adventure World of Sir Edmund Hillary* series], Peter must have been seventeen or eighteen, and almost every day I could hear Ed say to him: "On the 18th of February you are going to university." I could see Peter stick out his jaw and look away. Then the 18th of February came and went and Peter didn't go, and that sort of thing created huge tension.'

Such tension is part of what being father and son means. 'I think it was a normal father/son thing,' says Hilary Carlisle, 'trying to work out how to work together. It can't have been easy for Peter, wondering what he was going to do with his life, because being the son of a famous person is a hard thing to follow. It was difficult for Peter to find his niche, because there was always another adventure.'

To hear Peter tell it, it could never have been otherwise. 'The sort of person I am, in the environment we lived in . . . around that dining-room table we often had pretty exciting people come and join us for dinner. They would tell stories about where they had been with Dad.'

When Peter began to think about how much he would have liked to go on those adventures, it was 'the thin end of the wedge because, if you wished you had been there with him, well, maybe you will be next time. And of course he kept organising these expeditions. I started going as a junior member.'

'It is immensely difficult being the son of a hugely famous person,' says Mike Gill. 'There are expectations of you that you can't possibly live up to, because only one person could have climbed Mt Everest. There were other mountains to climb, but none of them mattered. No matter how much Ed might say that the most important thing [in his life] was helping out the Sherpas, a lot of other people have helped the Sherpas. Some not as well as Ed but they are not famous for it. Climbing Everest was a one-off.'

Peter could have avoided comparisons by choosing a completely different field of endeavour. But hearing him speak of the marvellous adventures and stories of adventure that filled his childhood makes it hard to imagine he could have seriously considered any other path.

Murray Jones disagrees. 'Sarah didn't do that,' says Jones. 'Scott's son became an ornithologist. It's not easy having famous parents, but he also had a lot of opportunities. We all did, because of Ed.'

Hilary Carlisle also believes that Peter was under no pressure to take on a life of adventure. 'It was Peter's choice. I don't think Ed was pushing him into things at all.'

Sarah's decision to become an art conservator meant she didn't have to confront many of the famous-father issues that Peter did. Just being the offspring of someone famous brings unwanted attention and numerous complications, but if you then go and emulate the famous parent's career, you are multiplying the potential complications for yourself.

'I think Dad gently tried to put the pressure on all of us to pursue careers that were more conformist, really,' says Peter. 'I don't subscribe to the idea "Just go and do what you are passionate about". You might be passionate about something, but what if you can't make a living? And is what you can make a living out of, as a 21-year-old, something you can support a family on and save for the future? He didn't discuss it in that detail, but he did want us to develop good careers.'

Ed, of course, did exactly what he was passionate about and nothing else. And he didn't have a proper job until he was in his sixties. Like many fathers, he seems to have had more conservative views about what his children should do than about what he himself should do. But if he was a 'do as I say, not as I do' father, it didn't work in Peter's case. Peter started a degree but, just like Ed before him, abandoned his studies—something he regrets.

'I certainly wish I had finished my degree, because it's something uncompleted and in the background,' says Peter. 'I am interested in natural sciences and virtually every day I read stuff about that type of thing because it does fascinate me. But I did a commercial pilot's licence and, while I didn't go on and develop a career in aviation, I completed that course.' Ed, it will be remembered, failed to be selected for pilot training when he was in the air force.

Ed was always proud that no one ever lost their life on any of his expeditions. Peter's successes have been coloured by more than one tragedy or near-tragedy. He nearly lost his own life, and another climber, Ken Hyslop, did perish in 1979 when he was attempting to climb Ama Dablam—the mountain that had proved irresistible to four members of Ed's 1960–61 HSME when they became the first to climb it. Peter's party was hit by an icefall, which killed Hyslop instantly.

Peter clearly had Ed's sheer passion for climbing and, indeed, the risks that come with it. As he puts it, 'When you are doing things that are very testing and challenging, especially ambitious mountaineering, you are trying to do something in a different way, a different route. It's not that we become complacent, but you go in there with a sunny optimism—we are the group and we have got the skills. We nearly pulled it off. We nearly did this new audacious route, straight up the centre of the west face of Ama Dablam— this beautiful mountain. And we were just about to go out at the 21,000-foot mark and bivouac for the night and we got clobbered.'

Fortunately, Ed was in the Himalayas at the time of the Ama Dablam incident. When he first heard the news, it was in a message from Elizabeth Hawley—who had told him of the accident that killed Louise and Belinda just four years before. Hawley knew one of Peter's party was dead, but not which one. It was a terrifying moment for Ed when he thought that he might have lost another child in an accident in this part of the world.

'He was immediately on the helicopter with me when I came out of there,' says Peter. 'We picked him up at Kunde; he came down to Kathmandu; he made sure I was in the hospital. There was a visiting American surgeon and so he was involved with that. And that was a demonstration of his caring. He wanted to do something; just standing and patting you on the back wasn't his style. But he could do something—he could be there in the helicopter, he could make sure he could be there to talk to the surgeon. That was certainly the Ed Hillary way.'

Peter first reached the top of Everest in 1990, with fellow New Zealanders Rob Hall and Gary Ball—making Ed and Peter the first father and son to have summited the mountain. Peter called Ed. The two had a brief talk, which Ed said was the longest they had had for some time. Peter told Ed he had been impressed at just how difficult the Hillary Step was.

Writing about the occasion in *View from the Summit*, Ed reflected that Peter's admiration for his feat of 1953 had caused him to feel 'a slight glow of pleasure'. He also marvelled at the new technology that made the call possible. But of Peter's achievement he expressed no opinion.

In 2002 Peter made his second ascent of the mountain. This time the phone call was filmed. Peter was wearing a hat with blue-and-white-striped shade, just like the one Ed's sister, June, had made and that he wore on the peak in 1953. But their conversation was less than inspired:

'Dad, it's Peter here—can you hear me?'

'I can hear you. How are you?'

'Good. We're on the summit of Everest—we've been here for 40 minutes. It's cloudy all around—amazing outlook, Dad.'

Peter had had other adventures in between, often marked by the sort of conflict Ed went out of the way to avoid on his own expeditions.

'In 1991 Peter and I were doing the traverse of the Himalayas and we were having tremendous difficulty getting on,' says Graeme Dingle. 'We met Ed at Kunde and stayed there for a while. Peter seemed a bit grumpy, and at one stage I said, "Hey, Ed, can you give me some advice on getting on with Peter?" He said, "No, I can't help you." That really surprised me at the time. It meant that he would probably have to compromise and he didn't want to do that. Years later, when Peter went to the South Pole, the guys [Peter] didn't get on with came to me and said, "Can we talk to you about this?" I said, "No, I can't help you." I kind of understood then.'

Dingle and Peter had many disagreements during their historic traverse. As Dingle tells it, 'Peter can be quite volatile, very stroppy. He could storm out at times, when we would be climbing, and I didn't cope with it.'

Though the two never came to blows, 'I felt like it at times,' says Dingle, 'but if it comes to decking your climbing partner, that's the end of the road. So I suffered some enormous emotional agony trying to get through the whole thing. Peter is a very, very determined person as well, just as Sir Ed was.'

Dingle—who, with his climbing experience and close acquaintanceship with both men, should be a very good judge of these things—has high praise for what Peter has managed to achieve in his own right. It's a sentiment echoed by John Hillary. 'Peter is tough but he is focused. There are a lot of people who have determination, but it can only happen to one in a million people that it comes together. Peter has done really well and I admire how he has handled himself and his life.'

Peter did really well indeed to survive a storm on K2 in 1995 that took the lives of his seven climbing companions. The group was well on its way to summiting the world's second highest mountain when Peter developed an intuitive sense that something was wrong. With the weather taking a turn for the worse, he decided not to carry on; and he was the only survivor of the terrible storm that beset K2 that night.

He also did well to survive the attempt to retrace Captain Scott's doomed 1912 journey by skiing to the South Pole and back with two Australians, Eric Phillips and John Muir, in late 1998. Compared to his father's relatively jaunty trot to the Pole, this was a hellish journey that dissolved into bitterness. During the 84 days it took to get to the Pole—after which they were flown out—the party endured fierce storms, painful frostbite and hunger. Some sort of temporary insanity or 'expeditionary madness' seems to have developed among all three. Peter suffered hallucinations.

The relationship between the two Australians and Peter collapsed. Within the narrow confines of their shared tent, the other two managed to shun him. They accused him of being not up to the demands of the trek and, in contrast to his father's reputation, not being a team player.

'I think I was the team player,' says Peter. 'I don't accept that at all. These things can become incredibly intense. There were some tensions, if you speak to the members of Dad's expeditions to Antarctica—they were there for 15 months. If you go back to Captain Scott, Amundsen or any of the other polar expeditions in between, it is a very testing environment. The ice trek wasn't one of my successes for sure. I do feel that, on most of the expeditions

I have been on, the great thing has been the camaraderie, the times spent together waiting out the bad weather.'

In another paternal echo, it seems that, just as Vivian Fuchs had piggybacked on the Hillary name to raise funds for his polar exploit, so too had Peter attracted the sponsorship that got the trek going. Eric Phillips later wrote a bitter account of the affair.

'A number of months before I left, I realised that I'd made a mistake with Eric Phillips,' says Peter. 'But what could I do? I was the person who really organised the sponsorships, brought the money in. It was like it was almost too late to change. You can pull out and collapse the whole thing, or do you want to take up the opportunity? Going to Antarctica on a major expedition is an extraordinary thing to organise. So you hope there will be sufficient maturities in the group and [they] will approach it the way you would any business. The three of us were in business. It's not like we had to like each other.'

Sarah is in no doubt that her brother and father share very similar personalities. 'He is very driven and very active and has many things going on. Peter is very talented with public speaking; he's athletic; he's good at climbing.'

Dingle sees in Peter—and Sarah—a 'tremendous blend of both their parents. There is a bit of the artist; quite a lot of the "considered opinion" of Ed.' John Hillary believes 'both Peter and Sarah have inherited his [Ed's] toughness'.

As it was for Ed, the toughest time for Peter and Sarah was after the death of Louise and Belinda. In his own personal variation on the strategy Ed employed to cope, Peter found some comfort in communal activity. 'With most of my expeditions there were great friends, great times, fabulous adventures. I think that was a coping mechanism because the relationships on these expeditions are very fraternal. I mean you are brothers in arms out there, you rely on each other, you are telling stories. If someone bursts into tears in Auckland city, people will say, "I think we need a psychiatrist." Up there on the mountain you go, "He's had a tough day," because he has. It's a very testing place; people are scared. Emotions bubbling to the surface is okay because it's that sort of place. But in the city it's not okay, because everyone should be able to restrain themselves and be composed. So one of the things that drew me, going on those climbing trips, was that you let your emotions go.'

It's impossible to imagine Ed expressing such sentiments. He was uncomfortable talking about emotions at the best of times. Tom Scott reports Ed disliking the book Peter wrote about the disastrous polar trek because Peter talked about feelings in it.

Yet there were other occasions when Ed and Peter seemed like almost the same person. Either could have made the following statement about adventuring: 'If you take on a major challenge, that makes you feel a little anxious and a little fearful, and you are challenging yourself. It's not a pushover, and you know you are going to have difficulties.' (It was Peter.)

Throughout most of his life, Ed seemed slow to express admiration for Peter's achievements. It may have been the primal 'old bull' problem, in Pat Booth's phrase—feeling that the young male was going to replace him. There is no reason to think his intense competitiveness didn't extend to his own son. Fathers and sons are naturally competitive.

Or it may have been that he simply didn't find what Peter did that impressive. We know, for instance, that he didn't see much point to anyone else climbing Everest. When Peter set off to climb the west face of Ama Dablam, Ed wondered why he didn't take on a less difficult challenge. Perhaps Ed's attitude was a result of his inflexible candour and his refusal to say anything if he didn't really mean it. Or perhaps Ed was trying to stay out of the way and let Peter get on with his own life.

'I've always felt, as far as my son's adventurous activities are concerned,' Ed told *HARDtalk*, 'that it's really entirely up to him. If he asks for advice, which is very rare, I might say I give him what good advice I can. But I really feel that he has to meet his own challenges and overcome them, which he has done very successfully.'

Peter himself is generous in praise of other mountaineers. 'Some of the best young climbers are pushing standards still,' he says. 'They find better ways of doing things—that's one of the exciting things about alpinism I think—there's just endless opportunities.' But Ed 'was a very hard person to get praise out of,' says Mike Gill, 'particularly for his children to get praise. It was really hard, I think. He was that "man alone" sort of guy.'

Ed was at his trademark candid best in a magazine story where he said that he was pleased about Peter's first ascent of Everest because 'it was obviously important to him . . . but personally I'd like to see him spend a little more time at home involved with his family and normal activities'.

CHAPTER 12
POLITICS

New Zealanders on the whole prefer that people keep their opinions to themselves—unless those people are being paid for their opinions. There is an underlying belief that you can't admire someone you don't agree with—and contrariwise, that you can't agree with someone you don't admire personally. In more evolved societies, public figures of many kinds are welcome to contribute their opinions to a general debate in the interest of advancing ideas and generating productive discussion.

Percy Hillary's son was always going to have strong political views. Here the generations were in accord. It was Percy's passion for social justice that inspired Ed's, which was then fostered by experiences such as the encounter with the poor Fijian boy during the war and his exposure to the low standard of living in the Third World countries he had visited. Neither father nor son was a free-market enthusiast. Both believed that governments had not just the ability but the duty to help those less fortunate to get out of the economic mire. Neither would ever accept that the world had to be a place in which a few people lived lives of great material comfort while a far greater number struggled to eke out the most basic of existences.

In *Nothing Venture, Nothing Win*, Ed lists the issues that caused him most concern. He deplored New Zealand's poor foreign aid record, and the international poverty gap; he was opposed to nuclear testing anywhere, sporting contacts with South Africa and his home country's enthusiasm for deifying athletes; he supported abortion law reform and family planning; and he took a keen interest in conservation issues. It wasn't just that his views on these issues were left-leaning liberal—it seemed the only issues on which he held strong opinions were ones that appealed to liberals.

One of Ed's trademarks, as kindly described by Tom Scott, was his unflinching candour. If he believed something was true, he would say so without the benefit of sugar coating. That this would cause him problems publicly was not likely to stop him. That it also could hurt those around him—well, that was regrettable, but if the thing were true he was going to say it.

So in 1967, when he spoke to a group of Auckland secondary school head prefects at a Rotary Club-sponsored lunch, he made honesty and candour one of his themes. He took the opportunity to implore these future leaders, when their turn came, to 'bring a little more honest-to-God morality into politics and government at all levels nationally and internationally. It horrifies me the way a head of state can one moment deny vehemently that his country is carrying on some particular action, and then a couple of days later and with complete calmness admit the whole thing.'

As the first president of Volunteer Service Abroad (VSA) in New Zealand, he encouraged his young audience to give up some time to working to help those less fortunate. And he lambasted the 'expediency and just plain dishonesty of utterances' prevalent in government.

From this distance it's hard to see anything wrong with an exhortation for honesty in public life. Yet the reaction of the then prime minister, Sir Keith Holyoake, was so strong that Ed had obviously touched a nerve. At a subsequent function organised by the VSA, the country's leader pointedly ignored the Hero of Everest.

But Holyoake earned a gold medal in cheek-turning compared to one of his National Party successors as prime minister, the pugilistic, small-minded Rob Muldoon. Ed's hatred of bullying was as strong as his passion for social justice. Nearly everyone interviewed for this book, when asked what annoyed Ed, mentioned Muldoon in their first breath and politicians in general in their second.

After one of Ed's semi-regular pleas for a greater government commitment to foreign aid, then finance minister Muldoon rose to the bait. 'Sir Edmund,' he said, 'knows as much about economics as I know about mountain climbing.'

Ed was annoyed. 'Actually, I know quite a lot about economics,' he told Tom Scott later. Indubitably more than Rob Muldoon knew about mountaineering. According to Scott, Ed also 'followed global politics closely. He was informed and curious about lots of things—medicine, health, sanitation, forestry.'

'Muldoon was quite vicious,' recalls Ken Richardson, a high-ranking public servant and diplomat who would observe Ed—and many prominent political figures—at close range off and on over the years. A brief foray into politics by Ed made him a confirmed enemy of Muldoon, and brought the adventurer more public criticism than anything in his life, apart from the South Pole debacle. Bill Rowling had become New Zealand prime minister by default, following the death of the charismatic Labour leader Norman Kirk in 1974. A man whose private abilities were far greater than any public impression he was able to make, Rowling was easy meat for Muldoon, and Labour supporters were desperate for a way to boost his image, even if it was only by creating charisma by association.

Television journalist David Exel attempted to come to the rescue when he led the formation of a group called Citizens for Rowling. These were prominent people who were happy to back the Labour leader in public—as much, it has to be admitted, out of distaste for Muldoon as enthusiasm for Rowling. The prominent figures included businessman and baronet Jack Harris, law professor Geoffrey Palmer (who went on to become prime minister briefly in 1989 and proved to have even less charisma than Rowling), Paul Reeves (an Anglican bishop who became governor-general of New Zealand in 1985) and Ed. Citizens for Rowling published newspaper ads and a booklet; and the words they used were as personal as anything Muldoon had ever uttered, if not more so.

In a historical footnote, Ed nearly became governor-general before Reeves. During Muldoon's subsequent time in office and two years after the Citizens for Rowling campaign, Keith Holyoake was appointed governor-general. Rowling, still leader of the Opposition, denounced what was seen as a political appointment and said that, were he in a position to do so, he would have appointed Ed as governor-general. This only served to embarrass Ed further, as it called into question his motives for backing Rowling in the first place.

Rowling knew nothing of David Exel's campaign until the last minute—and it was a failure. The reasons most frequently cited are that Rowling was beyond saving; and that the electorate reacted badly to being advised how to vote by a self-appointed group that was seen as élitist. Muldoon's tenure as prime minister ended in 1984.

'Anyone from the Citizens for Rowling campaign never got any government appointments at all,' says Richardson. 'That was Muldoon—he was very vindictive.'

Ed's stature was such that he got off lightly compared to others involved, including Exel himself. 'David Exel couldn't get work in New Zealand TV,' says former cabinet minister Judith Tizard, a member of the Labour Party dynasty. 'He had to go to Australia. It was a vicious and calculated attack on them all coming from Muldoon. Everything around Muldoon was rancid.'

Muldoon may not have been able to affect Ed's career, but he still managed to find an elegant way to exact his revenge, according to a story told by mountaineer and long-time Himalayan Trust member Norm Hardie. 'During the Kirk government years, a move was made for New Zealand to look into establishing an Everest National Park,' says Hardie. 'Two government staff went on a reconnaissance, and I went on behalf of the Trust. We made a favourable report. Kirk died, and in the Rowling years the park began with New Zealand government funding for five years and the inference a further five would follow.'

Then came Citizens for Rowling and Rob Muldoon's ascendancy to the prime minister's office. 'The Everest Park funding was allowed to go its promised five years, then stopped. The Himalayan Trust had no government support and some firms that might have been Trust donors were reluctant to show support, knowing the venom of the Muldoon revenge.'

The charge of being élitist alone would have been enough to make Ed regret his participation. People who are seldom criticised tend to develop a hypersensitivity to it, and Ed received so little negative commentary during his career that it seems to have been ill received whenever it occurred. Again, this trait is not unknown among people who are happy to dispense criticism.

It's notable that, despite high public awareness of the affair, Ed never referred to it in either of his volumes of autobiography, let alone attempted to explain what he was thinking. But no one could misinterpret Ed's views on issues, which were always consistent and clear.

'Ed always said he was a social democrat,' says friend and fellow adventurer Murray Jones. 'And he always believed in those traditional values New Zealand had before [the free-market experiments of] Roger Douglas. The greatest thing he could give to the Sherpas was education and health and, when you think about that, it's the greatest gift you can give anyone.'

'I thought [Citizens for Rowling] was a bad mistake,' says Booth. 'Although an ingenuous one. He hadn't grasped that he was not the beekeeper who could be called in by a local committee and give his support for a new road.'

According to Mike Gill, Ed had been annoyed by Holyoake's negative reaction to his Rotary lunch comments 'and with the Bill Rowling thing he realised he'd made a mistake. I think Louise said "I don't think you should do this," but he did and it was a mistake. Ed learnt from that sort of thing and he kept his head down.'

He may have kept his head down, but he didn't keep his mouth shut. Ed remained outspoken. If anything, the experience taught him to choose his moment and to avoid anything that linked him to party affiliation. Ironically, according to Tom Scott, he had been approached to stand for National in his home suburb of Remuera—the bluest of blue-ribbon seats—in the euphoric post-Everest years. At the same time, Judith Tizard is convinced his heart lay on the other side of the House: 'Ed was passionately Labour,' says Tizard. 'He was absolutely passionate that the point of being a New Zealander was giving everything a go and being entitled to do anything. He saw that as the heritage he had from the first Labour government.'

Labour Prime Minister Helen Clark became a good friend of Ed and June's late in life and was a neighbour at Waihi, where the

Hillarys had a weekender. Because of that, says Scott, and because David Lange sent him to India as New Zealand high commissioner, the Labour Party thought he was theirs and the National Party thought he was Labour's too. In the end, says Scott, 'he was above party politics. If Labour had a better foreign policy in terms of aid, so be it. But [National's] Don McKinnon admired him enormously and helped do things for Ed. People would claim ownership, but Ed needed the goodwill of all the governments to continue his aid work.'

Ed almost became involved in one of the great New Zealand protests of his lifetime—the campaign against French nuclear testing in the Pacific. 'There was Peter Mulgrew, me, Ed,' says Graeme Dingle. 'One time, we were really drunk on Scotch whisky. We made a pledge that the next day Peter would get a ship and we would sail to Mururoa to protest against nuclear testing. The next day, when we were all sober, I was the only one who still wanted to go ahead. I was really pissed off, but I was much younger and didn't have the same level of responsibilities. So they reflected on the promise and decided it wasn't a very good idea after all.'

Tom Scott brings the story of Ed's disinterestedness in the matter of party politics up to date: 'Most of Ed's friends in America were Republicans. Ed said: "We can't discuss politics because I don't agree with them, but really nice people can have strange views. You can't generalise." He judged people on how they behaved personally. The fact that Republicans were raising huge amounts of money for people on the other side of the world made them decent in Ed's book.'

CHAPTER 13
INDIA

In 1985 at the age of 66, when many people have chosen to retire, Ed started work at the first regular job he ever had, as New Zealand High Commissioner to India, Nepal and Bangladesh.

In 1982 the increasingly erratic Prime Minister Muldoon, following a disagreement with the Indian Prime Minister Indira Gandhi at a Commonwealth Heads of Government Meeting, had decided to close down New Zealand's high commission in New Delhi. The reason given was that New Zealand needed to save money. The Indian Government did not reciprocate, instead noting, somewhat cattily, that 'it understood the financial difficulties of the New Zealand Government and hoped that the mission would soon be reopened'.

His first snub having failed to wound sufficiently, Muldoon's government then announced that it planned to sell a plum piece of vacant Delhi land in Chanakyapuri, the diplomatic nerve centre of Delhi. India had given this to New Zealand twelve years before as the site for a new building.

Relations had been pushed as far as they could go without collapsing altogether, but within a year—and before the land could be sold—there had been a change of government in New Zealand. When Labour's David Lange—an enthusiastic Indophile—became prime minister, restoration of good relations between the two countries was a top priority. 'David was very keen,' says Lange's first wife, Naomi, 'knowing India and knowing so many people over there and they do amazing things with trade—he was just very keen to get it reopened. David thought it was crazy just to ignore them.'

Who better to mend the fence than Ed Hillary? 'He was the obvious choice because Ed was loved by the Indian people because of his work in Nepal. The Indians thought the world of him; he had a great rapport with them . . . All the Indians knew who he was and how great he was.'

It might have seemed obvious, but it could have been disastrous. Ed was indeed adored by millions of Indians, but he would not be working with them every day. He would be representing New Zealand at a diplomatic level. And diplomatic was not a word that had often been applied to Ed. He was easily bored, and diplomatic functions usually have an element of boredom built into them. And he would be dealing with career diplomats who were set in their ways and possibly resistant to being saddled with an adventurer in the top job. But he was no stranger to bureaucracy in this part of the world, having survived the negotiations that ensued after the illicit climb of Ama Dablam. It remained to be seen how well Lange's masterstroke would actually play out— if Ed took the job.

The phone call has become part of the legend. Ed answered it and the prime minister identified himself.

'David who?'

The prime minister was unimpressed but ploughed on and invited Ed to his Auckland home, where they would discuss the possibility of him taking on the role. Ed described himself as 'flabbergasted'.

While Lange's son Roy made the tea, a nervous Ed seemed most concerned with whether or not the job came with a car. He was an old India hand, but not at this level. Lange explained that there would be more than one car, plus a large staff. 'I don't think Ed had any idea of what it would involve,' says Naomi Lange. 'You learn on the job. There are other people taking care of things, but I think he was used to taking care of things himself.'

'What do you want me to do?' asked Ed.

'I want you to do precisely what you think is right,' said Lange. As a job description, it was quintessential Lange—expansive, imaginative and very short on mundane detail.

Ed had felt the burden of his grief for Louise and Belinda lighten somewhat in India during the Ganges trip, notably when receiving a blessing from a young Hindu priest at Varanasi. Interviewer Maggie Barry, discussing the appointment in the 2007 *Listener* interview, asked whether India had a healing effect on him. 'I suppose it has,' said Ed. 'I've never particularly thought of it in that way. But if an occasion occurs which I'm sad about, then I think India has a warming effect—and I'd go there tomorrow.'

Ed's other major concern when considering the job was that he would be allowed to absent himself to carry out his aid work in Nepal, and Lange was happy to agree to that.

There was one other slight speed bump: June. The two were now so close that the thought of a long separation was not a happy one. Ed wanted June to accompany him but, true to form when it came to intimate communication, couldn't bring himself to ask her. She was left to intuit his feelings on the matter. In the end she suggested the arrangement. After another phone call to Lange, checking whether it would be all right for Ed to take along an official companion—which it was—everything was settled.

For the media in New Zealand, June was coy. On a visit home during which she was planning to organise another of her group treks to Nepal, she was asked about marriage plans by the *New Zealand Woman's Weekly*. She and Ed had been in India less than a year at this point. 'I have frustrated other journalists, so I may as well frustrate you too,' responded June. 'I am Sir Edmund's official hostess, official companion, that is my designation in India. In fact, my identity card even has OC printed on it.'

She went on to clarify: 'Louise Hillary was what I would like to have called my best friend. Peter, my husband, was in the Antarctic with Ed. We were a foursome for donkey's years so it [the role as companion] seems to fall into place quite happily. In India, I am Sir Edmund's official companion and socially that is totally acceptable.'

Indians are conservative in matters of personal morality and that attitude extends to New Zealand high commissioners and their partners. Family friend and former governor-general, Dame Cath Tizard, is sure that the locals would have been more comfortable if the New Zealand High Commissioner and his consort had arrived united in holy wedlock.

'I don't think people said, "You can't come to this function unless you produce a marriage certificate,"' jokes Ken Richardson, who visited Delhi with David Lange, 'but the Indians have been for centuries under a very Victorian regime and maybe they inherited a lot of those attitudes. But of course it is gone now. The rumour was that the Indians would prefer them to be married, but I've never seen anything in writing.'

It's not clear why—given that they did get married eventually—the pair did not formalise things at this point. They may not have been ready, but the likelier explanation is the one that Ed expressed freely on the occasion of their nuptials in 1989: it wasn't necessary. He couldn't see the point. They were fine as they were. And at least this way, when they finally did get married, it wasn't so Ed would be eligible for a job.

Other diplomats expressed envy—they said they would have liked to have brought their secretaries, but hadn't been allowed.

'He was really pleased she was going,' says Hilary Carlisle. 'But I think the relationship cemented more to the possibility of a long-term relationship in India. They were a great team in India; they worked well together.' And, somewhat romantically, every morning they could they walked together in Delhi's beautiful Lodhi Gardens.

Their de facto status created some problems for the old India hands, but when they annoyed Ed by relegating June to the background when he presented his credentials to the president, they created a problem for themselves.

Ed adjusted well to the intricacies of diplomatic etiquette in general, though he struggled somewhat in Nepal when he presented his credentials there. Not only did he have to cope without the support of June—women being prohibited from the occasion—but he had to leave the royal presence walking backwards. 'I don't know much about backing out,' he said.

Naomi Lange got to observe Ed at work—and the drawing power of the magic name—in the early days. 'Ed seemed like he was in full control. He was a beacon. People would go to the High Commission for functions and there would be more prominent people there because it was him. You need a name to do that—it is a huge country. New Zealand is a minnow and overshadowed because of our size in the Commonwealth. That's why Ed was so important. So Ed spent a great deal of his time travelling, hosting functions and just talking about New Zealand. He took the flag to various parts of India.'

Ed stayed in the job for four and a half years. He turned up at the office every day, taken by his driver, and with the help of his PA dealt with the correspondence, requests and invitations. He often went home for lunch and returned to the office before heading out again for one or two evening functions.

Ed was the familiar face that businesspeople were thrilled to see at trade talks. If the government really wanted to impress somebody, the high commissioner might take them on a trek. He could also turn his hand to judging an International Mango Festival, if called upon. 'If the Foreign Minister of India wanted to discuss some-thing about New Zealand,' says Ken Richardson, 'Ed would have to front up. He couldn't send a deputy.' Which might sound like a tall order for the 'ex-beekeeper from New Zealand'. 'I don't think it came easy to him,' says Richardson, 'because he was basically a shy person. There are very few people, except those who started off with diplomatic lives and rose through the ranks, who can master the art of diplomacy. The best thing to do is to keep your mouth shut half the time.'

Keeping his mouth shut wasn't Ed's forte, but in this case he grasped the essentials and grew into the position quickly. If ever he should have failed at something in his life, it was this—a role for which he was apparently professionally unsuited—but in fact he had far greater failures on mountains than he ever had at the New Zealand High Commission in Delhi.

'He had great speech-making ability, so he was a wonderful guy to have along,' says Gill, who also got to see Ed in action when Mike Dillon was filming him. 'He didn't have to do subtle diplomatic manoeuvrings about arranging a treaty between China and Nepal. I think Ed increasingly quite enjoyed being in Delhi.

I think if you are in the limelight all the time, you miss it when it's not there.'

After Ed's death, Pat Booth received a letter from a woman who remembered seeing Ed in India. 'She was at the airport and Ed was wheeling a New Zealand climber, who had been injured, up to the plane. She thought that spoke a lot about the relationship he had—not just with fellow climbers, but also with anyone in trouble.'

Peter Hillary wasn't surprised that he was able to adapt to the job. 'I think as a young man he wouldn't have been an appropriate choice,' he says, 'but later in life he had the ability to speak, to meet all sorts of people, be a tactical thinker about how to solve various problems. He was also a very sophisticated operator dealing with people and cultures.

'He had techniques. If he didn't know exactly what was going on, Ed had a very congenial way of just sitting back and letting things move around, if he didn't understand what they were talking about, instead of putting his foot right in it. I think he was often quite good at thinking "I will just quietly sit back on this one."'

Both Peter and Sarah acknowledge, though, that Ed was there because of the power of his name rather than the quality of his diplomatic skills. 'Obviously, in an embassy,' says Sarah, 'you have all sorts of other staff who deal with trade and those areas of expertise. They needed Ed to get back in.'

'Dad could assist in various areas,' adds Peter, 'but in terms of breaking the ice and getting New Zealand back into one of the biggest, most important countries on earth with diplomatic representation, it was pretty phenomenal.'

As he had with other endeavours, Ed combined prodigious planning with a capacity to make things up as he went along. As the titular head of the High Commission, he met regularly with diplomatic assistants for briefings. 'He took advice,' says Tom Scott.

'He wasn't arrogant. "What should we do?" "That sounds good." If he thought he was right about something, he took a bit of shifting. But he was a reasonable, intelligent man and the Indians were delighted.'

Ed's name had been revered in India for more than 30 years by the time of his appointment—worshipped by many as, if not a living god, then at least the reincarnation of a god. The Indians were ecstatic to have him there. Other countries with diplomatic representation in Delhi might have had more trade power, more geopolitical influence and more money to throw around; but New Zealand had Ed Hillary. As Mike Dillon noted: 'It's very clever to have a god as your high commissioner.'

He was also popular for what he wasn't. 'If you look at the history of high commissioners,' says Richardson, 'invariably they have been politicians.' Skills, Richardson seems to suggest, were the least of it. 'He was welcomed everywhere. They just laid out the red carpet for him. They vaguely thought he was part Indian.' In local eyes, the choice also reflected well on India—New Zealand had gone from treating Indian diplomatic relations with utter contempt, to paying it the ultimate compliment of sending its greatest citizen to live among them.

Ed had been in the job less than a year when Tenzing Norgay died. On this occasion, he and June did ignore the advice that he not try to attend the funeral because of political unrest in the area. As they headed towards Darjeeling, Tenzing's home, accompanied by an army captain and driver, their way was blocked by an angry crowd. The captain told the mob who was in the vehicle and why, and hearing the name was enough. The crowd parted to let Ed and June through.

One important initiative carried out under Ed's supervision was the commissioning of new buildings for the vacant lot at

Chanakyapuri. Christchurch architect Miles Warren was given the job of designing the new complex. The imperial English architect Edwin Lutyens was responsible for the look of New Delhi—having based his designs on ancient Mughal architecture. Warren's design in turn mirrored this look.

Ed and June made suggestions as work progressed, but the couple never got to take up residence in the Warren building, which did not open until 1992. For a time, while their official residence was being renovated, under June's supervision, they lived in the Sheraton Hotel. When they finally moved back, June described their kitchen as being the same size as her small Auckland home, but she was thrilled to discover local craftsmen who could make furniture to her requirements.

June took her role as official companion seriously. By all accounts, Ed could no more have managed his work in Delhi without her than he could have lifted himself out of his old depression single-handed. 'June was extremely careful to be at Ed's side all the time,' says Richardson. 'I noticed also—and this is always a difficulty for famous people—that people came up to them and expected them to know who they were; and June invariably knew. I have heard her on a number of occasions saying to Ed as she saw someone approaching them—even me—she would say, "Do you remember Ken?" I don't think Ed would have got past first base in India as high commissioner unless he had had that support from June.'

Hilary Carlisle agrees: 'June did a fantastic job with setting up the High Commission there and making it work, managing that social stuff. They were very popular diplomats and of course they used to take other diplomats on trips, expeditions and adventures. They were a good team in India . . .'

June even learnt to drive—a hair-raising pastime in Delhi—putting to rest any last doubts about whether she had the courage and adventurous spirit to match Ed's own. And the Indians took to June in this role, just as their counterparts had taken to her in Nepal. 'Effectively, she was the Memsahib who had to manage the servants, the entertaining, the catering,' says Gill. 'It was a big job, very important, and June did it well. She is also organised, and she probably liked the entertainment side of it. You didn't have to peel the spuds, but you had to tell them what to cook. I think she was very proud of what she did there.' June reported that, when she got back to New Zealand, she had forgotten how to make a white sauce.

One obligation was that every country had to turn up at every other country's national day. With 130 nations represented, that was a fair chunk of the social year automatically taken care of.

June did her bit representing New Zealand. In 1985 she had told the *Woman's Weekly*: 'I'm very nice to Cook because we haven't had a meal from him yet. He doesn't speak English unfortunately, but I have communicated with him and explained the sort of things Sir Edmund likes, which are basic things like a good stew and plenty of potatoes.' But by 2007, speaking to the *Listener*, she seemed to have come a long way. She then recalled: 'It was a big help that the Indians were very, very kind to us. And I enjoyed the Indian women. I was on all sorts of committees, which was an experience I'll never forget. Everybody is the chairperson on a committee in India.'

She described those years as 'probably the happiest time we had together'.

CHAPTER 14
TRUST IN TURMOIL

The Himalayan Trust, Ed's informal charity which started its life modestly with the aim of helping the Sherpas of the Solukhumbu with some basic facilities, has grown into a multifarious, sprawling collection of organisations around the world, including the Hillary Himalayan Foundation, the American Himalayan Foundation, the Sir Edmund Hillary Foundation of Canada, the Australian Himalayan Foundation, the Himalayan Trust UK (founded by members of the 1953 expedition) and the Sir Edmund Hillary Foundation of Germany.

There is no doubt that his ongoing humanitarian work in Nepal was seen by Ed as his greatest achievement. He intended it to be his legacy; and he went to some lengths to put that on the record when being interviewed by Mark Sainsbury in 1991. 'When the camera was rolling, Ed made a solemn declaration: "When I kick the bucket, I don't want memorials. I don't want statues. I just want the work to continue."'

But Ed's vision for what the Trust would be after his death—and who would be running it—would be a major source of contention.

As well as continuing Ed's work, the New Zealand-based Himalayan Trust also provided a means by which family conflicts were acted out. Various parties took on the roles of antagonists, peacekeepers and bridge-builders with varying degrees of success. These currents swirled around Ed but, so long as he was alive, they were contained because of respect for him and his reputation. After his death, they spilled into the open and brought many long-concealed differences to a head.

The greatest question around all this is why Ed Hillary, the leader of men who could inspire others to do so much, could not settle a simple, all-too-common family squabble. But the fact is that, for the last few years of his life, he was simply too old—these were the years when people made efforts to keep conflicts away from him.

However, the conflict between Peter and June—which was Ed's problem too—had been there from early on. Unfortunately, each of the three people concerned was unusually strong-willed. It was no doubt easier day-by-day to pretend it didn't exist, rather than confront this difficulty. Ed's absences in India and Nepal also meant it could simply be ignored for long periods of time. And Ed was never comfortable expressing himself except in letters, or in a burst of temper. He may simply not have known what to say. However, failing to deal with this conflict would lead to deep divisions within the Himalayan Trust; and a public squabble after his death that did nothing to enhance Ed's legacy.

June had been there at the start of Ed's work in Nepal. In early 1961, visiting with Louise and other wives of members of the Himalayan Scientific and Mountaineering Expedition of 1960–61, she had literally put in some hard yards, completing a 290-kilometre trek. And when she and Ed were together, just as Louise had done before her, June practised hands-on humanitarianism.

'At Phaplu Hospital,' she told ABC's *Foreign Correspondent*, 'I remember painting the whole kitchen, inside the cupboards. The paint was awful and the brushes were hard to work with.'

The pace never let up. Ed had insisted that they be allowed time in Nepal to carry on their work while he was high commissioner in India. Travel was a constant. 'Ed and June went around the world fundraising year after year,' says Murray Jones. 'It was bloody hard work. Ed was quite nervous with travelling. He got anxious about that sort of thing. He wanted to do everything right, so it was quite hard work for him as he got older.'

Peter and Sarah, too, had been involved with the Trust from early days. It was widely, but by no means universally, accepted that Peter would take over leadership of the Trust in due course. June, for example, was another strong candidate.

'Many of us thought it was Peter's legacy anyway,' says Graeme Dingle, 'so that created a tension. Had they got on, it would have been clear to June that that's what should have happened in the long term, but the other thing that we can't possibly know is what Ed said to June.'

According to Tom Scott, who remains one of June's greatest admirers, there were also external cultural obstacles that had to be taken into account. 'June has been astonishing and done great work,' says Scott, 'and the Sherpas know that. But it's a patriarchal society and Peter Hillary is the son and they probably would prefer Peter—he's younger and fitter—to take over. And Peter would like to take over.' Peter echoes Scott's opinion. 'A lot of people in Nepal, which is a very traditional community, see it in that light. I have a lot to offer in that area. I am on the boards of most of the supporting foundations. I have done a lot of fundraising for the Himalayan Trust. I work with the British and German foundations as well.'

Like any organisation populated by the sort of people who can get up mountains and to the South Pole, the Trust has always been subject to numerous internal tensions driven by the strong personalities involved. One of its first directors to resign, in fact, was Peter Mulgrew who, as we have already seen, was agitating for a more rigorous, business-like approach to the financial side. He had been one of the original members when the Trust was founded in 1966. 'Mulgrew put demands on Hillary,' says Norm Hardie, a 22-year veteran of the Trust. 'He told Ed to put things in order, have proper minutes in the meetings. Mulgrew was the first of the original board members to withdraw and it was Hillary's lack of business ability and poorly run meetings that caused all of it.'

Hardie himself remained with the Trust till 1988. 'I resigned over the differences I had with Ed and Rex . . . In doing so I said to Ed I hoped the other old ones would also retire (meaning Rex) and that young workers would replace us. I had said in the past that Ed should have taken Peter on early American tours so that continuity would occur, and that Peter should be on the board. Nothing came of my wishes.'

According to a story in the *Sunday Star-Times*, in 2002, in what seemed to outsiders an unpaternal gesture at best, Ed prevented Peter from gaining control of the Trust board. If Ed, as he had said, did not approve of dynasties, he was going out of his way to demonstrate to what extent he disapproved. 'That was ludicrous,' says Mike Gill, who blames the tension between June and Peter for the move. It was tension, he says, that sometimes rose to the surface.

Some commentators suggest that it is odd for Peter yet again to want to do something his father did superbly well; but in fact, it's the most natural thing in the world. No one queries the logic of a Ford going into the automobile business, or a Rockefeller into banking, or a Redgrave into acting.

Old friends and allies—people whose bonds had been forged on high adventures with Ed—suddenly found themselves having to take sides. 'I have taken Peter and Sarah's side,' says Mike Gill, adding that 'pretty much' everybody else has too. 'I was a very good friend of Jim Wilson's; but he is a very good friend of June's, so we had a bust-up. June expects loyalty. With June you are either in, or you are out.'

From 2002 June held sway at the Trust, supported by many of the old guard, such as Jones and Wilson, who continued to support her after Ed's death. 'Jim and I are only doing what we think Ed would [have wanted],' says Jones. 'He told people he wanted June to carry on with his work with the Himalayan Trust, and she did. That's why we supported her, because she was carrying on Ed's work; but others couldn't accept that for whatever other reason, and I don't really understand their reasons.'

Underpinning the family conflict were some serious philosophical differences about how the Trust should work and in which direction it should go. Even Hilary Carlisle felt some things needed to be changed. 'The Himalayan Trust was done on Kiwi ingenuity—No. 8 wire,' says Hilary, 'and actually in the modern world it needed to be more robust. The accounts are complex, with all the different currencies—the Nepalese accounts, the Americans, the Canadians, the British accounts. Imagine doing it by hand.'

'Peter wanted to corporatise everything,' says Murray Jones, 'and Ed didn't believe in that. Ed did all the work himself, apart from Betty Joplin, his secretary, and he wasn't getting any money from it. There was no middle man getting a cut. He was a one-man band.' (He was actually a two-man band—Mingma Tsering *was* the Himalayan Trust in Nepal.)

'There was no office as such,' adds Jones. 'It was just his study. Ed did most of the books, but in the end he got Doug Page to do the books.' But some weren't happy with Page. When Mike Gill questioned his ability, 'I couldn't get anywhere. I would talk to Ed about it and he'd say he'd get back to me. When he did, he would say, "No". So that was the way it went.'

One key difference of opinion was over who should direct the way the aid was used: Should the money be handed over to the Sherpas to do with as they saw fit; or should the projects be driven by the Trust?

Ed had always taken the first view. The Trust only existed because he asked Sherpa Urkien what the locals needed that he might be able to provide for them. And even in the days when he carried around his sack of cash, that cash was distributed to people based on what they told him they needed. He never changed his view.

'June and Ed decided,' says Jones, 'and this was [Prime Minister] Helen Clark's policy at the time, that it was for the local people to run their aid work. [The New Zealand Government makes a substantial contribution annually to the Himalayan Trust.] The day of the white man over there is long gone. And some people in the Himalayan Trust in New Zealand cannot accept that. They feel they have to be the guiding white man and give them the guiding hand. Ed and June never accepted that. The Sherpas are perfectly capable of organising and doing things their own way. All we are is the go-between, between the New Zealand Government and the Sherpas.'

In Peter's view, however, New Zealand has a lot to offer, not least because of the half-century of experience the country has in providing practical assistance in Nepal. 'You've got the high-altitude physiological research, the first schools and hospitals, the forestry—all this expertise coming, much of it from this country. The Department of Conservation joined forces with Nepal to set up the Mt Everest National Park, and that was something Dad was very involved with. So New Zealand has been involved in the Mt Everest bit of Nepal for 60 years and we should maintain that involvement. There are a lot of opportunities for us to continue our work in health and education.'

Ed didn't cope well with criticism or being challenged, and he didn't cope well with the disagreements within the Trust. They might appear to have washed over him, but he clearly knew what was going on because he prevented Tom Scott from getting drawn into it. Scott recalls: 'June Hillary said, "Tom and Averil should join the Himalayan Trust."' Ed said, "Oh there's no need for them to do that." He virtually told Averil and I not to get involved. He knew what a mess it was turning into.'

As he got older, Ed's ability to cope with being challenged grew less and less, effectively pre-empting any criticism. 'You learned not to say stuff,' says Hilary Carlisle. 'I am in strategic planning and governance. I had a lot to contribute to the Himalayan Trust which was about modernising it, but Ed didn't have the energy for it. I think Ed and his friend Zeke [O'Connor, president of the Sir Edmund Hillary Foundation of Canada] got worried about the ongoing program of the Himalayan Trust and what would happen. He got more and more concerned about how he would continue it. He couldn't cope with that change, so in a way it was easier not to change.'

Ed never stopped working as hard as he could for the Trust but, as he got older, the strain began to show. 'It was a big effort to do the fundraising,' says Carlisle. 'He couldn't have done that without June. He would spend a week to two weeks doing the accounts, manually of course. And then in the Trust meetings people would challenge the numbers and Ed would get upset. June didn't like seeing him upset, so she would try and manage the situation. It [was as though] that stuff wouldn't get discussed because he would get upset. He had hearing aids. He could cope a bit in a group, but for a three- or four-hour meeting it is really tiring if you have people speaking in all directions. June really looked for ways to reduce his stress.'

As time went by, it might have been expected the Trust would get on with its work free of family tensions. But the 2011 ABC-TV's *Foreign Correspondent* program contained criticism of June for something that had occurred back in 2004. The program focused on an occasion three years after Ed's death, when Peter and June attended the 50th anniversary celebrations for Khumjung School. It included an interview with Jim Strang, who had run advanced teacher training for the Trust in Nepal from 1997. But June had felt that enough was enough and in 2004 Strang's funding had been turned off.

'We did it for six years . . . four years . . . I can't remember,' said June. 'They felt that was good enough. It was the same with the forestry—we did that for a certain time. I think that's the way to do aid, really.'

'This [decision] is incredible,' said Peter on the program. 'We've got this remarkable person, a team of teachers, a great need.'

The depth of the conflict is apparent, not only from what was said onscreen. When Peter and June are seated for one of the ceremonies, they are only centimetres apart; yet there is no eye contact, not a word exchanged. Two adults—a man and his father's widow; a woman and her late husband's only son—cannot bear any contact. Peter and June live in adjoining, upper-crust Auckland suburbs and have travelled thousands of kilometres from there to get here, yet it would seem each pretends the other does not exist. It was during this visit, June said later, that she decided to step down from the Trust.

ABC reporter Eric Campbell put into words what many in his audience would have been thinking. 'It's fairly obvious today there is something of a rift between you and Peter Hillary,' Campbell suggested.

'I don't want to discuss that,' answered June. 'No. Peter Hillary has created a rift between him and me.'

'I think up there with that ABC documentary,' says Peter, 'I know it was dawning on June she had to do something and she has. She resigned. But when you think about it, she was at the helm for a short time. She turned 80—I think she made a good decision.'

Jim Strang's teacher-training program was almost immediately picked up by the Australian Himalayan Foundation in 2005 and expanded over the following two years. It now involves almost 300 schools. The New Zealand Trust still resources schools, but doesn't conduct training.

In a telling contrast to June's view of 'the way to do aid', Peter led Eric Campbell's cameras away from Khumjung to a nearby town—just a short way from one of the trekking hot spots, but far enough from the beaten track for it not to benefit from tourist money and not to be as favoured by the Himalayan Trust as other areas. The poverty is extreme, especially by comparison to the area around Khumjung. 'A lot of the challenges people had in Europe centuries ago are their challenges,' Peter says.

In 2003 the New Zealand Government set up a new Annual Funding Arrangement with the Himalayan Trust. In 2007, the year before Ed died, New Zealand Aid conducted a review of the Trust. For all the fretting about the Trust's attitude to professional accounting rather than Ed's old-fashioned approach, the organisation emerged relatively unscathed from an inspection. The review found that:

One of the main strengths of the work of the Trust is that it has focused on helping people to help themselves, rather than importing ready-made solutions. The Trust occupies a position of influence in Solu Khumbu and has a great opportunity, and a certain responsibility, to accomplish all it can, to the highest possible standards, while continuing to leave the development agenda in the hands of the people of Solu Khumbu.

The report identified as key issues that 'Solu Khumbu's fragile environment is under increasing stress due to growth in tourism' and 'The Trust faces the challenge of finding and developing a new generation of leaders for both fundraising and project implementation.'

The question of leadership would certainly be a focus of interest in the next few years.

Things came to a climax following certain events that occurred after Ed's death. In its 2011 newsletter the Trust noted the celebrations of its 50th anniversary and recorded its international achievements for the year. Included was this anodyne paragraph:

> After the celebration of 50 years' work of the Himalayan Trust Senior Founding Members of the Himalayan Trust New Zealand, Lady June Hillary, Jim Wilson, Murray Jones, Douglas Page, David Hayman and Rebecca Hayman resigned and the responsibilities passed on to the Chairman Dr John Heydon, Diane McKinnon, Secretary Dr Kobi Keralus, treasurer Sarah Hillary and Dr Mike Gill and the new members of New Zealand Himalayan Trust Council is expected to increase in near future with amendment of Himalayan Trust New Zealand Constitution [sic].

The Trust issued a statement at the time of these resignations but it couldn't seem to decide how it felt about June and her allies falling on their swords:

> Whilst all of those who have stepped down have made a hugely valuable contribution, over long periods of time, to the work of the Himalayan Trust Board, there is great significance in Lady June and Jim [Wilson] each ending their long-standing membership of the Council. Both Lady June and

Jim were foundation members of the Council, when the Himalayan Trust Board was established in September 1966, and each has had an unbroken chain of involvement in the work of the Himalayan Trust Board since that date. Murray Jones has also had a very long association with the Himalayan Trust Board.

But the move came as no real surprise to those close to the main players. 'June and the other trustees could see the writing on the wall,' says Graeme Dingle. 'There was no future. The trust had to be reinvented and to do that it needed some modern ideas.'

The two camps had become irreversibly entrenched in their own positions. There was no Ed around, whose feelings both sides wanted to spare, and inevitably blood would be spilt. Some family members had tried to bridge the gap between the two sides, but the distance was too great.

'The whole thing is very, very sad', says Murray Jones, who is still of the opinion that Ed wanted June to head the Trust. 'What he wanted to happen in the Himalayan Trust was laid out, but other people thought they knew better and wouldn't accept it. Like many people in the Himalayan Trust, I have been torn to pieces because of my loyalties to Ed and I don't want any more to do with it.'

By choosing not to speak publicly, June has passed up a chance to defend herself. She has obviously been pained by much that has happened, not just since Ed's death but in the years leading up to it. Now, she does not even have the consolation of her husband's presence to make her plight more tolerable. She has left her defence to others in her 'camp'; but they, like her, have little stomach for what seems to be a tawdry epilogue to a life of devotion and service.

'It wasn't just about the Himalayan Trust,' says Jones. 'It goes way, way back. I am well aware of the problems. I find it quite disturbing to see the people who have put so much into the Himalayan Trust, like June, unfairly maligned. But she can't really defend herself. If she says anything, it makes the spat even worse and sometimes you have to rise above it. But, it's torn us all apart and we really want nothing to do with the Trust anymore. Ed would be so upset as to what's happened. I was there when Ed said he wanted June to carry on with his work, but other people couldn't accept that.'

Several months after the resignations, Sarah was adamant the Trust was in good hands. 'June and her family resigned but we are an interim committee council. We were in the middle of updating our new constitution anyway before they resigned. We expect a new constitution completed by next year, then we can start the process of electing new council members.' Sarah suggests the new system will be both more flexible and more secure, lessening the possibility of someone getting and keeping a stranglehold: 'Anyone can be voted on. The chairman will be elected for the year—there will be no permanent positions.'

The Trust is important to Sarah, she says, 'Because our parents put so much work into it and because we think it has been very successful; but there is still a lot more work to be done.'

June's move was reported as far afield as the UK, where the *Guardian* newspaper reported the reaction of Mary Lowe—wife of George Lowe and secretary to the Himalayan Trust UK. 'We can't hide the fact that Peter and June never got on,' Mary told the *Guardian*. 'They're both tough characters. June's been working for the Himalayan Trust for fifty years. It's just the right moment for her. It's a new start.'

CHAPTER 15
STORY APPROVAL

Ed was given credit for many exceptional qualities in his lifetime. Not least of them—though among the least commented on—was his skilful use of the media to achieve his ends. And because the ascent of Everest occurred just before television was about to take hold of the world, Ed and the medium developed alongside each other.

The camera, as we have seen, was crucial to proving that the ascent had occurred. If there had been no camera with Ed and Tenzing, the world would have had to take their word for it. Given how much trouble some people had accepting their achievement, even with photographic evidence, the difficulties of convincing them without it can only be imagined.

They took some convincing themselves. It's been observed that, from the late 20th century on, something only exists if it is reported in the media, and it seems Ed was no exception, as he explained to the US Academy of Achievement: 'We did have a little radio at base camp, and somebody tuned into the BBC in London and the announcer was just describing the coronation of Queen

Elizabeth II, and then he broke into the coronation and said, "We have great pleasure in announcing that the British Everest expedition has finally reached the summit of Mt Everest." And then, almost for the first time, I felt, "My God! We've climbed the thing and we've had authoritative support from the BBC in London that we've done it!"'

No one lasts long in the media unless they can provide a good soundbite, and Ed got off to a great start with 'Well, George, we knocked the bastard off.' It was easily the equal of 'One small step for man, one giant leap for mankind' in memorability, if not in philosophical depth. But it was the very laconic Kiwi shoulder-shrug of it that charmed the world (even if it did not charm Ed's mother, Gertrude—she was appalled at her son's vulgarity and made her feelings known about it). And then there was the tantalising ambiguity of 'we'—was that the Hunt team, or was it Ed and Tenzing?

There were no cellphones in 1953, and the expedition did not have its own radio. James Morris, the UK *Times* correspondent attached to the team, realised that the announcement could be made to coincide with the coronation if he acted quickly enough. He raced down from the camp to the nearest radio, at an army post at Namche Bazaar, to get the news to London.

On 1 June, *The Times* received Morris's coded message: 'Snow conditions bad hence expedition abandoned advance base on 29th and awaiting improvement being all well.' In a gesture that can only make contemporary journalists nostalgic, they shared it with other media, and people everywhere awoke to read on the front page of their papers that Britons had beaten the world's mightiest mountain.

Ed bore the inevitable confusions in reporting with good grace. The *Daily Mail* headline was typical: 'The Crowning Glory— Everest Conquered. Edward Hillary plants the Queen's flag on the top of the world'. Ed didn't mind the lack of any reference to his nationality. He identified happily as a British subject then— though he was a New Zealand citizen. But he did resent being called 'Edward'.

Back home, the *Auckland Star* was ready to go to press with fulsome front-page hosannas to the coronation of Queen Elizabeth II. The monarch was quickly relegated to the back of the paper so that room could be found for a much more important piece of local news.

Before he had even left Nepal, Ed had an encounter with the press that he found extremely distasteful. An Indian reporter, claiming to be acting on behalf of an English newspaper, offered him a large sum for an exclusive story. (The large sum was £8,000 in *Nothing Venture, Nothing Win* but had grown to £10,000 by the time of *View from the Summit*.) How, Ed asked, did the reporter think Ed would feel if he did such a thing when there was an agreement in place (with the London *Times*) covering the whole expedition?

In a piece of sophistry that would have done any of his 21st-century equivalents proud, the reporter said the people he was acting for had felt the size of the sum would have been sufficient balm for Ed's feelings. Ed raised a fist—he describes himself as still capable of violence in those days—and the journalist scuttled away.

While in England on the way home, Ed stayed with his sister June in Norwich. 'It was quite a disruption in our family,' recalls June's daughter Hilary. We had a lot of paparazzi after him. He had to sleep at our neighbours' down the road, which we could get to without people seeing, going across the back fences.'

And it wasn't just Ed who was affected. Back home, *Auckland Star* journalist Pat Booth was the first to bring the news of the ascent to Ed's parents, Percy and Gertrude. In some ways ahead of his time, before he knocked on the front door, the canny Booth primed his photographer to snap at the crucial point.

It was Gertrude who answered. When told the news, her face lit up in an open-mouthed, wide-eyed, unrepeatable combination of shock, joy and relief. And the moment was captured in a photo that ran in the paper the next day. Although low on dignity, it could not be beaten for emotion and impact.

Percy was livid—he was one of those people who still regarded private lives as private. The day the picture ran, Booth returned to do a follow-up interview. 'And I was ordered off the property by Percy. "That was a disgusting photograph of my wife that you published," he told us. So we got the photographer to take a new photo and we were allowed to stay.'

When Ed came back, Booth went out to the house and knocked on the door again. Percy opened it. Booth recalls the conversation:

'Could I have a talk to Ed?'

'Sir Edmund is in bed.'

'That would make a great picture.'

'It would be disgusting to take a picture of a knight of the realm in bed.'

Finally, Booth says, 'I heard this voice from upstairs. "Oh for God's sake, let him up, Dad."' And the *Star* got its photo of Sir Edmund Hillary in his striped pyjamas having a lie-in and reading his mail. 'He was a total novice with the press at that point,' Booth comments now. When the reporter later turned up unannounced on Ed and Louise's wedding day and Percy tried to throw him out yet again, Booth accepted it was a fair cop and went quietly.

In general, though, when it came to the media, Ed obliged. Perhaps it was unfortunate for him that he didn't realise at the start that he could have said no to the media. Instead he established a policy of access that he was more or less stuck with for the rest of his life.

One of the more remarkable records of those early days is a National Film Unit short called *Hillary Returns*, in which the conquering hero is hailed in his hometown. It begins with Ed and George's triumphant return to Auckland on a Sunderland flying boat, met by a crowd of thousands at Mechanics Bay. Already some romantically contrived fictions were being spun around Ed. This, the narrator tells us, is not a civic welcome but 'a truly spontaneous greeting' by admirers and friends: 'All the excuse they needed was they were fellow New Zealanders.'

It's hard to believe the greeting was all that spontaneous, what with a public address system for Ed to use and a National Film Unit crew on hand to record it.

It is notable in this footage that Ed's voice does not have its characteristic booming quality—this must have developed later. The film ends with an on-camera interview, which would surprise no one. What is surprising is the choice of interviewer—Ed's brother, Rex. No two brothers, unless their relationship was thoroughly dysfunctional—and Ed and Rex's wasn't—ever had a conversation like this. The two stand outdoors dressed in suits, with their hands firmly planted in their pockets.

'What do you consider were the highlights of your trip to Everest?' asks Rex.

'I suppose the main highlights were the actual bits on the mountain itself,' replies Ed. 'The ice fall perhaps—[was] the most interesting thing ... some of the bits of ice hanging overhead made a rather keen impression on us. And for me especially the last summit effort from the south col to the top. The effort I'll remember for some time.'

'What about that rock step—that was fairly steep wasn't it?'

'It wasn't too bad. I was a bit worried about it at first and thought that we wouldn't get up it, but fortunately there was a crack between the ice and the rock. I was able to get into this and wriggle my way up it.'

'I believe George Lowe did a very fine job.'

'Yes, George did extremely well. He did a jolly good job on the Lhotse face, which ranges from about 22 to 25,000 feet . . .'

'Now, after climbing Everest, what are your impressions of the New Zealand mountains?'

'Well I still think the New Zealand mountains are extremely fine ones. In fact we have wonderful mountains here. They have so much snow and ice on them that they are wonderful training for the Himalayas. The weather here is so bad that we have to be extremely careful with our climbing. [. . .] In the New Zealand alps you have to use very sound judgement and a considerable amount of care in our very difficult conditions.'

What is remarkable is how many of Ed's media trademarks are already in place—the gentle downplaying of achievement, while leaving the audience in no doubt of that achievement; the sincere allocation of other credit where it is due; and, of course, the conclusion with words of praise for home. The last is not especially Hillary-esque; no New Zealander would dare do otherwise.

Ed learnt a lot about handling the media on the Everest party's lecture tour of the UK. During this he found time to provide a foreword to the *Auckland Star*'s serialisation of John Hunt's book *The Ascent of Everest*. In a covering letter to Pat Booth—by now a de facto Hillary editor-at-large—he said that he had learnt overseas that 'New Zealand journalists are much more pleasant to deal with than the overseas press vultures'.

Ed's view of his persona was consistent and often repeated: 'The press and the public have created an image of Ed Hillary, hero and explorer, which simply doesn't exist. They've painted a picture of me as a heroic type, full of enormous courage, tremendous strength, undying enthusiasm and all the rest of it. But it's all really just a story that's been written up in the newspapers.'

He is right, but it might be more accurate to say that the image he describes is half a portrait. It omits the foibles and frailties that Ed knew make a whole man.

Ed also seemed to know from the start how to have his photo taken. Judging from many that have appeared in various media over the years, he spent a lot of time gazing up at distant mountaintops. And if there was so much as a mound anywhere near where he was being photographed, Ed would have to ascend it. In a fascinating account of Ed's trip to the Pole the year before he died, which appeared in the Christchurch *Press*, John Henzell described what happened when he went to take a photo of the 87-year-old: 'his eyes met mine and suddenly narrowed, his jaw firmed and any frailty that had previously been apparent disappeared in an instant'.

Not every photo of Ed told the whole story however. At least one well-known shot, though not a fiction, misrepresents what was happening. In Louise Hillary's *Keep Calm If You Can*, there is a photo of Ed and Ron Hayes with a magnificent bull moose that Ed has shot in Alaska. It's a standard triumphant hunter composition, in which Ed stands proud and smiling, his hand resting on the beast's antler, which is half a body length.

In his first volume of autobiography, *Nothing Venture, Nothing Win*, Ed says his reaction to the killing had been one of 'shame and disgust'. He knew how to handle a gun—he had spent a season back home as a young man shooting deer to make some money— but he was not a hunter at heart. His inner sense of fairness could not accept a contest between a firearm and a wild animal. But for the requirements of the photo, he was able to summon up a classic victory grin.

Ed's first book, *High Adventure*, appeared in 1955. There followed books on the Barun Valley expedition, the Trans-Antarctic Expedition, the attempt on Makalu and the building of Khumjung School.

Nothing Venture, Nothing Win appeared in 1975. It was a thorough retelling in serviceable prose of each of the stories that had had their own books; and it detailed—with more frankness than might have been expected by anyone who didn't know him—the vicissitudes of his childhood.

'Ed kept a tight rein on his story,' says TV journalist Mark Sainsbury, who got to know him in the last 20 years of his life. 'I think he was conscious of what his legacy meant and how it could be used.'

Ed's own writing didn't quite do his narrative skills justice. 'When he sat down and wrote,' says Tom Scott, 'it was a job and he did it. He was a good planner of expeditions: you sit down, it has to be done. He adopted the same approach with a book. He'd work out the structure and bang it out. But he didn't write like a raconteur. Even with his speeches he had a plan and would achieve it. It wasn't a case of "off the cuff and drop in a few bon mots". Yet if you were around at his place and having a few drinks and casual conversation he would be great. He was funny.'

Naturally, with exploits and a character as conspicuous as Ed's, stories sometimes took on a life of their own. A French newspaper once reported that Louise was going to climb Everest with an all-woman team, 'to prove she is as good as her husband'. Following his success at the Pole, Ed was nominated by the *Baltimore Sun* to be the first man sent to the moon. He would no doubt have been up for it, but instead he had to settle for meeting the man who did get the job. As a final example of spin, it's hard to beat the headline on the announcement of Ed's death on the website Cryptomundo, devoted to Sasquatch, the Loch Ness Monster and the like: 'Yeti hunter Sir Edmund Hillary dies'.

It wasn't just Ed himself who had to learn how to deal with the media. Much of Peter, Sarah and Belinda's early years were caught on film, and not just on 8-millimetre home movies to be watched with family: chunks of their childhood were witnessed by TV audiences around the world.

Louise refers frequently to the media presence in *Keep Calm If You Can*, her account of the family's year spent based in Chicago with a 70-day sortie into the Pacific Northwest and Alaska. 'Someone told me once Ed was a bit stupid and his wife wrote his books,' says Scott. 'Then you go and read his books and you read her books and you go, "Oh, no."' Louise seems to have been a more natural writer than Ed, able to wring anecdotes as easily from humdrum domestic details as from adventures in Alaska.

A constant theme in *Keep Calm* was the price of fame and, in particular, media intrusion, to which Louise seemed more sensitive than her husband—perhaps because she had three children to protect. She was to learn that when you have a sponsor—in this case, both the National Forest Service and Sears Roebuck—you still have to pay for what you get, albeit not in cash. When she found out that Sears would be filming the Alaskan holiday, she was horrified. 'I think it is only natural that the wife of a well-known husband should try to hide her identity,' she wrote; and she explained why, when she was on one occasion mistaken for a New Englander at a campground, she was happy. She was also happy to gather her brood and decamp when reporters found Ed and started throwing questions at him.

Soon, the children had 'become very allergic to photographers and at the first sight of them would start acting like convicts, covering their faces with their hands. [. . .] We resolve that the less the children saw of the Press, the better it would be for them and from here on Father had to hold the fort and answer all the questions while Mum and the kids crept off somewhere.'

Almost inevitably, however, like a pride of lions being stalked for a nature documentary, the Hillarys became accustomed to having their observers around and almost forgot they were there.

Ed's life and adventures continued to be a subject of fascination—and ratings for TV networks—for the rest of his life. In the early 1970s he worked with director Roger Donaldson on *The Adventure World of Sir Edmund Hillary*, a series in which he and other stalwarts such as his son, Peter, and Graeme Dingle would dream up hair-raising escapades and carry them out on film with great aplomb.

In 1986 there was less aplomb when Ed was the focus of an episode of *This is Your Life*, a popular program in its day, in which the subject was ambushed unawares for a live TV retrospective in which figures from their past were given the opportunity to reminisce nostalgically about them. The supporting cast that had been organised for Ed's show included luminaries such as David Lange and Rajiv Gandhi. The key to the show's success was to take the victim by surprise, which in Ed's case proved to be more difficult than for most.

The show was to be filmed at Auckland's Sheraton Hotel, and diplomat Ken Richardson was employed as decoy. 'My job was to get Ed without any knowledge to the hotel,' says Richardson. 'I told him I thought it was an interview about his position as high commissioner in India. He had been interviewed many times at press conferences by dozens of journalists, so he was relatively relaxed. We went to the hotel room where the make-up girl made him up. I was told at four minutes past eight, after the adverts, that the host, Bob Parker, would come in, open his book and say "Ed Hillary, this is your life—follow me."'

But for once, Ed was not comfortable and he said to Richardson: 'Look I have had interviews before and people tell me what they are about. The producer or director would tell me what they expected. Where are they?'

'I don't know. I am not the organiser.'

Minutes ticked by and an unpleasant silence reigned.

'He was quite angry,' recalls Richardson. 'I saw this stern side of him, which comes out in his biography.'

'For God's sake, Ken, what the hell is happening? What time is this man coming?'

'I think this is just about India . . . I think.'

'I don't have it at my fingertips, the trade between New Zealand and India. If they ask me that, what am I going to say? I will look stupid. It can't be about Everest—there's been a lot done about that. They could ask me about what I do day by day.' He complained that it wasn't fair.

Eventually, Parker appeared and Ed was, if not appeased, at least apprised of what was going on. And so the show played itself out.

'That side of him was a new thing,' says Richardson. 'He wasn't shouting at me, but he was just mouthing away. No one wants to look stupid.'

A few years later in 1991 Ed was the subject of stories spread across three episodes of the nightly *Holmes* show. His friend, cartoonist and writer Tom Scott, was travelling to Nepal with Ed and suggested reporter Mark Sainsbury go along too, to do a story. Ed, of course, saw this as an opportunity not so much to appear on TV as to raise awareness of the work of the Himalayan Trust.

The show's origins were somewhat macabre, and Tom Scott gets the credit, as Sainsbury explains: '[Scott] said, "You should do something for the *Holmes* show. He could drop dead any minute. Someone needs to get this stuff."'

The irony was that Ed nearly did drop dead while doing the show.

Sainsbury was as blunt as Scott when he pitched the idea to his bosses, who approved it. At that point he went to the library to see what old footage there was; and he realised that 'every ten years or so someone like me had done exactly the same thing'.

Ed was, as always, accommodating; he never seemed to find a TV crew intrusive. Sainsbury soon recognised that the relationship was mutual: 'He knew the value that the media would give in terms of doing his stuff, so he went along with it.'

Ed (and June, too) appreciated Sainsbury's humour and lack of deference. Ed also knew exactly what the media required. Sainsbury was most impressed by his ability, at over 70, to find new angles on subjects that he had talked about, in some cases, hundreds of times over the years. The producer had initially been worried about coming up with something fresh and new, but Ed always seemed to have a nugget in reserve that no one had heard before.

But then Ed developed a bad case of altitude sickness during a visit to Nepal—his old foe. 'That was terrifying, having pitched this thing on the basis he might die . . .' says Sainsbury. 'I remember the doctor saying he was taking in as much oxygen as if he was at the top of Everest.' With June waiting anxiously alongside her husband, they tried to get a helicopter to take the whole crew to Kathmandu. As Sainsbury narrates, 'By evening the weather had deteriorated and so had Sir Edmund. The Kiwis maintained a vigil in his room, desperately rebuilding the oxygen equipment from the local Hillary Hospital to keep him going. In the worst of the weather Mingma Tsering, Hillary's loyal Sherpa friend, led a party out in search of more oxygen as remaining supplies fell perilously low. By first light he was back, just in time.' Eventually the helicopter got through and Ed quickly recovered at a lower altitude.

Sainsbury became known as the key Ed contact. For the world media, who didn't understand how New Zealand works, this could have some amusing sidelights: 'Although his phone number was still in the phone book, I used to get calls from CNN: "We would like to get in touch with Sir Edmund Hillary. Can you help?" "Have you looked in the phone book?"'

Ed might not have been in control of his lungs at high altitude, but he still decided who told his stories and how. For the 40th anniversary of the ascent, Pat Booth was approached by a publisher to write a biography of Ed. Booth, of course, had been there at the start, although this was news to the publishers when he told them. In fact, in the interim Ed had invited Booth to go along on the Makalu attempt, but the Press Association had decided it was too expensive. He described it as 'the best story I never wrote'.

Booth's biggest challenge with the new project was Ed himself, who 'proved more difficult than one could imagine'. Booth rang Ed and explained he had been commissioned to do a book.

'I can't see much point in it,' said Ed. 'I write my own books.'

'Well, can I come and have a talk to you, anyway?'

'When?'

'Whenever suits you?'

'How about 3 o'clock tomorrow?'

The next day, at the appointed hour, Booth knocked on the front door and found himself being regarded with as much enthusiasm as a Jehovah's Witness.

'Yes?'

'Pat Booth.'

'Yes?'

'The book.'

'Oh, oh. Well, you'd better come in.'

Ed was intransigent in his unwillingness to cooperate.

'Would you be prepared to look at the manuscript after I've finished?'

'No. Don't want anything to do with it.'

With Ed out of the picture, there was no question of June being involved, and Peter and Sarah said no. Fortunately many friends, acquaintances and other family members made themselves available and Booth produced a sterling tome, *Edmund Hillary: The Life of a Legend*.

One of his sources was George Lowe, who provided some colourful memories. Booth says he later heard that Ed had challenged Lowe over some of the statements he made in the book, but Lowe reportedly rejected Ed's claim, saying: 'I never saw him. I never met him in my life.'

Ed did form close relationships with two biographers. The first was Tom Scott—cartoonist, writer and (some 20 years before he and Ed met) a fellow bête noire of PM Rob Muldoon. This could well have predisposed Ed to like Scott. Scott lists some other factors that may have helped the bond: 'No garbage. Hadn't climbed with him. Hadn't seen his aggression or ambition, or seen him grief-stricken. Sainsbury and I were clean and a lot younger and good humoured.'

The two first met when Ed was addressing a dinner in Canberra. Scott was brought on to introduce him and was inspired to make one of his better speeches, which in turn brought out something in Ed. 'When I sat down,' says Scott, 'his eyes sparkled and he said, "I'll have to lift my game. That was pretty good." I thought, "Oh, you are competitive." But he did give one of the best speeches I've ever heard him give.'

The two shared a few whiskies and lunch the next day.

'How come no one's made a movie of your life?' Scott asked.

'Oh, the right person hasn't asked.'

'I'd love to write it,' said Scott.

'You are the right person,' said Ed.

'Think about that. You've drunk a lot of whisky. I'll give you a call in January.'

But it was Ed who rang Scott, inviting him to Nepal on the trip that Sainsbury covered. Scott ultimately produced the four-part documentary on Ed's life, *Hillary: A View from the Top*.

The body charged with providing funds to bring New Zealanders' own stories to air—NZ On Air—had its doubts about the documentary; they wondered if Ed Hillary's life was interesting enough. So Ed, Scott and a representative of the TV network fronted to answer this simple question. 'I think it's been reasonably interesting,' said Ed. 'Tom would know more about that.' Somehow the writer talked up his project enough to get funding; and there turned out to be more than enough content.

Unusually for someone so jealous of his own story, Ed gave Scott complete freedom and access when making the documentary, even declining the opportunity for a preview. 'No, I'll watch it like everyone else.'

The documentary was finished in 1997. Scott had worked on it over six years and four visits to Nepal. 'Just after finishing the documentary Ed said, "I want you to write my biography. You know more about me than I know about myself."'

Scott suggested they write the book together. Ed's memory had undergone the normal wear and tear over the years; while an update to his 1975 memoir, *Nothing Venture, Nothing Win*, was long overdue, now almost 25 years later, this time he would need some help.

'I've just finished the documentary, Ed. I'm buggered.'

'If I can do it at 78,' said Ed, 'I think you can do it.'

Scott had no option. 'Suddenly I had Ed the taskmaster. He was writing chapters and sending them to me and he left all sorts of stuff out. I'd read his first book and all the *National Geographic* interviews at the time [of Everest]. What he said in interviews sometimes was much more expressive than when he was writing.' Scott pointed out some omissions to Ed, who replied: 'Oh well—you have a go at those and put it back in.'

Scott wrote up a few chapters, sent them off and hadn't had a response by the time he and Ed appeared on a radio program together—each in a different city—to promote the documentary.

'Ed's still on the line,' said the producer when the interview was over. 'He wants a word with you.'

'Gidday, Ed.'

'I'm not sure about this. I've read your stuff.'

'Yeah?'

'It's too good.'

'Oh. Thanks, Ed.'

'No. It's *too* good.'

'What's the . . .'

'You're a better writer than me. I don't write like that. It doesn't sound like me. I don't want you to write any more. Just supply me with the stuff I've forgotten and I'll put it in my own words.'

The result, *View from the Summit*, shows signs of different hands at work, with much of Scott's early chapters intact, and many of his reminders incorporated into the text as he had supplied them. As well as the updated material, some of *Nothing Venture, Nothing Win* has been rewritten, while there are whole sections from the earlier book carried across.

From Scott's point of view, Ed's decision 'meant the book I would have written myself has now been done. I can't ever write a book about the climb, because I've written it already. I thought, "shit—he's still competitive."'

Yet another anniversary piqued media interest as 2003 approached—it would be half a century since Ed and Tenzing Norgay got to the top. Among those to whom Ed gave interviews was John Martin Meek, a US writer and mountaineering enthusiast who flew to Auckland to record a video interview for the American Alpine Club. His interview showed that, despite the passage of half a century, Ed in some ways had got no further than when he started.

'Sir Edward,' Meek began.

'It's Edmund,' the great man corrected.

Meek recalls: 'I told him if he could please excuse me—I of course knew his name and blamed it on jetlag.' As if he hadn't done enough to risk offending Ed, Meek then asked: 'Sir Edmund . . . Has anyone ever questioned you about proof you were the first on Everest? Because I have done a lot of research, and so far as I can find there is no photograph of you up there.'

Ed—and June, who made lunch—were patient and polite. Finally, the interview complete, the Hillarys showed Meek how things were done in New Zealand. When he asked if June could call him a cab, she insisted on driving him back to the B&B where he was staying. Meek was so stunned he took a photo of June in the car, as if he might need proof such a thing had happened.

The last volume of biography with which Ed was personally connected was *Sir Edmund Hillary: An Extraordinary Life*, by Alexa Johnston. Billed as 'the authorised biography' and providing a thorough, careful recording, this could claim to be definitive, so far as describing Ed's achievements was concerned.

Johnston had come to know Ed as the ultimate ordinary bloke. A colleague of Sarah's at the Auckland City Art Gallery (as it then was), she met him in the most Kiwi of ways—borrowing a piece of garden equipment, a roller she needed to flatten some lawn. In 2003 she curated the wildly successful exhibition, *Sir Edmund Hillary: Everest and Beyond*, showcasing Ed's entire career. It included photographs, relics such as the Everest ice axe, one of the South Pole Massey Fergusons, replica Sherpa buildings, Ed's Order of the Garter and a plethora of other material. The exhibition toured to the US, Australia and Japan.

'I'd never been skiing,' says Johnston, of her qualifications for organising a show about Ed; but Peter and Sarah wanted the show to be put together by someone they knew and could talk to about it. She spent a lot of time at the Hillary home, trawling through the mountain of material that Ed had amassed and uncovering numerous forgotten items that rounded out the exhibition.

Johnston knew Ed was given to real slumps throughout his life, but found the elderly version anything but cantankerous or moody. 'It was endearing for an octogenarian to be still enjoying things.'

In the wake of the exhibition, a colleague asked Johnston when she was going to do the book. 'The thing that decided me to do it,' says Johnston, 'was the visitors book from the exhibition . . . there were all these unbelievable comments. People saying things like, "This makes me proud to be a New Zealander"; "It's incredible"; "I'm off to buy his autobiography". There was no catalogue—we hadn't had time. So I thought I'd try to do a book of the exhibition and went to see him.'

'Ed, I thought I'd like to do an illustrated book,' Johnston told him.

'I can't think of anyone I'd rather have write a book about me,' said Ed.

Only later, long after she had sent her proposal to various publishers, did Johnston learn that Ed had turned down such eminences as professional biographer and historian Michael King.

'I think I got though the back door by doing the exhibition,' says Johnston. 'It was going through all that material, looking at all the slides and finding so many he had forgotten about and, in a sense, bringing his life back to him again. He said, "I want to thank you for the way you've dealt in the book with June and Louise," because this is the thing he was constantly struggling with.'

CHAPTER 16
A VIEW FROM THE SUMMIT

As a consequence of living so long, Ed gave more than the usual number of retrospective, valedictory interviews and was subjected to more than the usual number of tributes. Having achieved so much in his early thirties meant that 50-year anniversaries rolled around regularly when he was in his eighties.

If anything could trigger one of his despondent periods, it was a bout of bad health. His health was erratic at best, and dismal when he spent time at high altitudes—something he persisted in doing far past the stage where it was comfortable. But given the problems he had had over the years—the stroke, the altitude sickness, malaria, to name a few—he kept in remarkably good health until not long before his death. He got tired. He forgot things. He had the problems anyone in their eighties is likely to have; but, because he was Ed, people found these everyday things to be noteworthy.

'Dad was in his seventies and although he was reasonably fit he actually went downhill pretty rapidly after that as a lot of people in their seventies do,' says Peter. 'He became isolated; he wasn't doing all the big stuff anymore. There was still a lot of interest in him because he was this huge personality who had this huge life, and they travelled extensively. But it wasn't doing the big expeditions and it wasn't doing the actual buildings—it was like social engagements.'

Ed said he never stopped dreaming of adventures. 'I'm past carrying out some of the wishes that I would have wanted to do before,' he told the *Listener*, 'but I still dream about what I would like to do if I was able to do so. You know, I'm nearly 88 and so obviously I'm a little bit on the limited side as far as carrying out exciting moments. But I still dream about them; I still spend quite a lot of time thinking about how I would like to do this or that.'

'He had a punishing schedule,' says Sarah. 'Tom Scott went on one of his tours and he couldn't believe the pace of the interviews, the lectures—it was pretty gruelling.'

Scott became friendly with Ed late in Ed's life, and he joked that, if they had met any earlier, they wouldn't have got to know each other at all because Scott wouldn't have been able to keep up with Ed.

Even the social engagements were planned like mini missions. 'He just had his systems,' says Peter. 'Even after the interviews and the dinners and he'd given the speech, he'd sign a few things, he'd say "hello" to a few people and then bang—he'd be gone. At 9.30 he'd be gone. Everyone would carry on, but he'd go to bed and the next day is another day. The systems enabled him to deal with quite a gruelling schedule.'

Nothing happened to improve relations between the various branches of the family. Hilary Carlisle says Ed was aware of the problem, but wouldn't deal with it.

'June is a different sort of person to what I would normally mix with,' says Peter. 'So, as so many families around this country would testify, you are there because of the relationship you have with him—not with *them* but with *him*. So you know everyone does their best, but sometimes there were good times and sometimes it was more stressful. I think it is not dissimilar to a lot of families. Unfortunately, if anything happened, it would be on the front page.'

It was never a chore for Ed to visit one of the Poles. In 1985 he was invited to the North Pole on a two-week visit in the company of Neil Armstrong, with whom he was often compared. As Peter tells the story, he and his father were having a cup of tea at the Remuera house when Ed said, 'Would you like to go to the North Pole?' Yes, he would.

The trip was an extraordinary gathering that also included the balloonist and adventurer Steve Fossett. Peter, who was in some awe at being in Armstrong's presence, and all too aware of what his father had endured over the years, fought the temptation to ask, 'What was it like on the moon?'

Peter told ABC Radio his father and the astronaut had amazing conversations, and eventually Armstrong began to talk about the lunar expedition, including the last-minute recalculations that had to be made to ensure a successful landing.

Armstrong, like Ed, had often said he was just in the right place at the right time—next on the list. Ruthless ambition had nothing to do with it. Having seen them up close, Peter concluded that both had made sure they were in the right place at the right time.

Both, of course, also uttered lines that went down in history. Ed himself practised a mild form of revisionism in later life when he supplemented the 'bastard' quip by saying to interviewers that he liked to think, not that he had conquered Everest, but that Everest had 'relented'. It was a much more carefully crafted, statesman-like and sententious response than the words he uttered at the time.

Ed continued his regular trips to Nepal, including the 1991 visit when he developed a severe case of altitude sickness. As Mark Sainsbury observed, Ed knew the score. Travelling at high altitudes was a calculated risk—or, more accurately, a miscalculated risk; but in 1991 he made a rapid recovery and gave the only explanation an adventurer could be expected to give: 'I have the alternative of lolling on a sun-drenched beach—something I find exceptionally boring—or going off to the Himalayas and meeting friends I've known for years and doing something which may have a slight risk, but which for me is very exciting.'

The older you get, the more funerals you go to. Ed attended the obsequies for his old opponent Rob Muldoon when he died in 1992, and even shed a few tears. 'I cry easily,' he told an interviewer. 'I wasn't one of Sir Robert's greatest supporters by any means, but there was something about him I had to admire all the same.'

Ed's admiration for David Lange was never in doubt, and when Lange died, Naomi Lange remembers Ed as a conspicuous figure among many notable New Zealanders at the memorial service: 'I was talking to Sir Ed while we waited for the service to start. [. . .] I think he was always the same with people—although of immense stature, he was able to put people at their ease by the way he spoke.'

In 1993 Ed travelled to Everest to celebrate the 40th anniversary of the expedition with the surviving team members. Tom Scott was there too. 'They were all up on stage,' says Scott. 'It was a bit like a Last Supper. All these old wizened men and one fairly erect and silver-haired—this Colin Meads figure towering over them all. He looked indefatigable and like, with a bit of training, he could do it again. They had their reunion photos and the Poms all had their Everest-issue jackets, which they had kept because they were historic. But Ed—and this is proof of his lack of historical vanity—had long since lost his. He had worn it beekeeping and it had disintegrated years ago.' The other team members' jackets looked as though they had been stored in archival conditions. Ed had to borrow one to wear for a staged photo with John Hunt.

The old imperial/colonial divisions could still be seen. 'The Poms had regulation army camps, with tents perfectly aligned and structured with their hierarchy,' says Sainsbury. 'The Kiwis were off to one side, a bit more ramshackle. The Poms had a mess tent and would dress up. Each side was totally different.'

Old political faux pas dogged Ed into his eighth decade. Tom Scott suggested to National Party Prime Minister Jim Bolger that a 40th anniversary dinner should be held in New Zealand as well. Bolger, citing Ed's Citizens for Rowling involvement, turned him down. However, Deputy Prime Minister Don McKinnon was more amenable to the suggestion and a dinner adequate to the occasion was held. Ken Richardson, who had shepherded Ed into his appearance on *This is Your Life*, was a frequent visitor to the house. Sometimes he would visit with Cath Tizard; other times on his own.

'People knew I had befriended Ed,' says Richardson, 'so they asked me to take books to be signed and I took one myself, which he would happily sign. On another occasion I had another book and I told June I would leave it in the letterbox. She phoned me and said "We are going to London for the Garter ceremony." I said "Okay." She said "I will leave it in the letterbox and if you are coming past you can collect it." So I did. There was another inscription and two of the five-dollar notes that have his face on, which he'd signed for me. That was quite moving for me.'

A tsunami of accolades came his way, none more prestigious than the Order of the Garter, the highest order of knighthood that the Queen can bestow. At the ceremony Ed marched in procession with his political polar opposite, Margaret Thatcher, with whom he had nothing in common except an interest in making their mark in remote locations.

The man who bridled at being knighted without his consent 42 years before was happy enough to accept this nod, though again there were difficulties. The honour, it seems, though gratis, would involve substantial disbursements. Ed rang Tom Scott and told him he was worried about how he was going to pay for it. 'I have to fly to London, get a coat of arms, find accommodation . . . Can you help me?'

'Yes, Ed, I'll fix it.'

When Scott hung up, he realised he had no idea how he was going to fix it. So he rang Richard Griffin, who was media adviser to Bolger at the time. 'Dick, Ed's got this great honour but it's really expensive. He's got to pay for a gown, get a shield designed. It's a lot of dough.'

'Leave it with me,' said Griffin.

About a week later, Griffin rang Scott, 'and it had all been taken care of. He'd spoken to a merchant bank . . . Air New Zealand. Ed was very grateful. He gave me the credit, but it was really Dick [Griffin].'

The Reserve Bank of New Zealand helped out by donating the fee for his coat of arms, which included an ice axe, a penguin and prayer wheels, plus the motto: 'Nothing Venture, Nothing Win'.

Ed was also a foundation member of the Order of New Zealand. Other honours that were bestowed on him in his lifetime included the Order of the Gurkha Right Arm, the Everest Medal in gold, the David Livingstone Medal of the Scottish Geographical Society, the American Geographical Society of New York Medal, the Belgium Le Soir Medal, the Geographical Society of Chicago Medal, the Hubbard Medal of the National Geographical Society, Washington, DC, the Cullum Geographical Medal of the American

Geographical Society, the John Lewis Gold Medal of the South Australian Branch of the Royal Geographical Society of Australasia, the French Geographical Society Medal, and the Distinguished Services to Geography Medal of the Geographical Society of Philadelphia, the Polar Medal and the Fuchs Medal of the Royal Geographical Society, London, the Patron's Medal of the Royal Geographical Society, London, the French Order of Sports Merit, the Order of the Golden Ark of the Netherlands, and the Order of Merit of the Republic of Poland.

Even his death didn't put an end to the recognition, with a posthumous Padma Vibhushan (Decoration of the Lotus), awarded by the Indian Government.

There was a fuss about the ownership of some relics being auctioned in 1998. It turned out that on Ed's Trans-Antarctic run in 1957, some items from Scott's and Shackleton's huts had been 'souvenired' by John Claydon and were to be auctioned at Christie's in London. The news offended Ed on many fronts. Most of all, when it came to respecting predecessors and their property, he was fiercely protective, although a ban on such souveniring did not come into effect until the adoption of the 1959 Antarctic Treaty, signed by the twelve nations then active in the area.

'Various members [of the expedition] visited the huts, as I did,' Ed told the New Zealand Press Association (NZPA), 'but I certainly never, ever took anything from them. We regarded them as a place of enormous respect really and I didn't believe there was any effort made to take anything from them.' Had he known, 'I think I could have completely stopped it. I was the expedition leader.' Ed thought the items should have been returned to the huts, but they were donated to the Scott Polar Research Institute in England.

Ed continued to exercise his accustomed candour well beyond middle age. Criticisms that had been muted in *Nothing Venture,*

Nothing Win were louder in *View from the Summit*, published in 1999. 'There are some things which I feel now I'm almost approaching 80 I can speak out a little bit more firmly on,' he told the BBC. 'I've always been careful not to say anything which might offend other members of my expedition. But now I'm not worrying too much about that, telling it like it was.'

He was asked less frequently who got to the top first, but the mystery surrounding George Mallory popped up from time to time, and was given new life when Mallory's remains were discovered high on Everest's North Face in 1999. But in the same BBC interview, Ed allowed himself a grunt of annoyance when the question of Mallory being the first man to reach the summit was put to him: 'Climbing friends . . . in the 1930s, especially Shipton . . . did not feel he got to the top,' Ed said. 'Who knows? The big thing is that this discovery of the body hasn't resolved the problem of whether Mallory got to the top or not. The only thing that will do that is if a camera is found and film is produced showing shots from the summit. One other thing I think all mountaineers will agree—Mallory was a heroic performer. You can't take that away from him. However, it's quite important on a big mountaineering expedition not only to get to the top but also to get safely to the bottom.'

The English mountaineering fraternity, in particular, has never quite been able to let go of all hope that Mallory was first to the top. Fortunately, Ed was not alive to hear about Jeffrey Archer's fictional account of Mallory making it to the top, published as *Paths of Glory* in 2009.

Ed was also publicly critical of the large number of people who climbed Everest annually, mainly because of the ecological impact they had. By the end of the 2010 season, 3142 people had summited. On the day Peter reached the top for the second time, in 2002, so did 78 other people. In a glaring contrast to the rigours of organising and preparing for the early reconnaissance expeditions and the Hunt expedition itself, an Everest expedition can now be booked by anyone with a personal computer.

'I don't think it's a very satisfactory arrangement,' Ed told the *Listener*, 'because the mountain has been covered with people. Some of them are climbers, some of them aren't, and so there have been quite a few deaths of people who aren't very knowledgeable. I tried to persuade the Nepalese Government to restrict the number of teams they had on the mountain, but they get a lot of money out of it—I'm afraid money came before sound advice.'

'There was an interview with Rob Hall and Gary Ball,' says Tom Scott, 'where they criticised Ed and said he didn't understand modern climbing. They were quite patronising and condescending. His era was over. Ed said people are going to die on these climbing trips. Everest should not be turned into a business.'

A friend told Scott that Ed came across as a fuddy-duddy in his response to Hall and Ball: 'I was defensive. I said, "I'll put my money on Ed. He'll outlive those two. Ed's knowledge is hard won." I had no basis for saying that. I was a bit knee-jerk. But within two or three years both had died on the mountain.'

'He was very hot on people paying 60,000 to go up,' says Mark Sainsbury. 'Ed thought this was wrong. One of the reasons was that you'd never be able to leave the climb.' In Ed's view, if two climbers are on a mountain and one is injured and likely to die, the other can leave. But if the injured climber has paid the other climber to be their guide, the guide has to stay. 'Once you start accepting money, you can no longer make the rational decision,' says Sainsbury. 'And that is exactly what happened to Rob Hall [who died on the mountain in 1996]. He could have got down—he stayed with his client.'

Kevin Biggar, who had had the good fortune to work in Nepal for the Himalayan Trust while a schoolboy, reappeared in Ed's life when Biggar and Jamie Fitzgerald were planning their first big adventure—competing in the Woodvale Atlantic Rowing Race. Ed always had time for a young person with an ambitious project in hand.

'Sir Ed came to the launch of our boat when it had just been completed, and spoke,' says Biggar. He lent his name as patron to the effort. Ed's support meant more than money: 'Having him there meant we got on TV. Having him as a drawcard to come to our launch was fantastic—it meant our sponsors came too. He spoke so well.'

When the pair decided they would walk unsupported to the South Pole, without supplies dropped along the way and taking everything they needed with them, they naturally thought of the world expert on madcap polar exploits and went to see him.

'He'd always open the front door,' says Biggar, echoing the surprise of many people that Ed treated his home just like a home. As June brought tea and scones, they told him about their plans for the crossing. 'He was dismayed that there were no drop-offs. He thought of his own trip, and his mission was the supplies—it was going to be 50 years since his. He thought it would be good to do it first. He had strong feelings about being first.'

Ed again agreed to support the mission. 'It was generous of him to associate his name with us. If someone asked me the same, I would do a lot more due diligence than he did.'

Ed had acquired a sort of secular semi-divine status at home by now, as Murray Jones couldn't help noticing. 'When they had the Hillary exhibition [the Alexa Johnston-curated *Everest and Beyond*] in Auckland Museum,' says Jones, 'when we came out, June was driving him and people would see Ed in the car. They would stop and start clapping at him. That was amazing. I'd never seen that before—genuine New Zealanders in Auckland.'

In public, his harshest words were reserved for those who failed to show the sort of old-fashioned chivalry and grace that was at the core of his character, especially up a mountain or down a crevasse. He had had this attitude from the start—in his description of the Ruth Adams rescue in 1948 there was never a hint of resentment at the situation in which he found himself. He summed up that affair by expressing his pleasure at having the opportunity to see some of the country's best climbers in action.

'He thought there was a lack of chivalry on the mountain,' says Scott. 'He was from an age where, if you came across someone dying, you would abandon your attempt and get this person down. [His contemporaries] were honourable men. They had a courtliness about them. Hunt was the most gracious man. None of those guys would step over a body.'

So when Mark Inglis, who in 2006 became the first double amputee to summit Everest, reported seeing the dying English mountaineer David Sharp on the climb but not stopping, Ed was incensed. There were some 40 climbers on Everest that day. Accounts of exactly what happened and what, if any, chance Sharp had of surviving differ widely. But everyone agrees Sharp was left to it.

'In our expedition there was never any likelihood whatsoever, if one member of the party was incapacitated, that we would just leave him to die,' said Ed. 'It simply would not have happened . . . If you have someone who is in great need and you are still strong and energetic, then you have a duty, really, to give all you can to get the man down and getting to the summit becomes very secondary. You can try, can't you?'

'The last person in the world who could have rescued anyone was Inglis on his two artificial legs,' says Tom Scott. 'He could barely get up there himself. To expect him to do it ... When I heard Ed, I thought, you don't need to say that.'

Ed's last great journey was in the year before he died—an odyssey to Antarctica to celebrate the 50th anniversary of the New Zealand presence that he had helped establish on that continent. Ed was very frail and very determined to make the most of what he certainly knew would be his last visit to one of the places he loved best of all. Attendant media were in awe; in each of them, their desperate desire to make the most of Ed's presence was waging a fierce war with their respectful acknowledgement that he might deserve to be left in peace.

But Ed didn't want to be left in peace. He appeared energised once he hit the ice. A promised 20-minute interview with accompanying media turned into 40 spellbinding minutes of anecdotes about his adventures there over the years. It got a standing ovation from the assembled journalists and others who had drifted in during the performance.

Finally, before returning to New Zealand, according to John Henzell in the Christchurch *Press*, he was granted his wish to spend a night in 'an old A-frame hut discarded by the Americans and instantly appropriated by the Kiwis to serve as the equivalent of a bach on the ice shelf. He wanted to spend his final night in Antarctica cooking dinner on the same type of Primus stove Scott used and just telling some yarns over a few tumblers of whisky.' Which he did.

Back home visitors were still welcome. Ken Richardson's last visit was just a few months before Ed died. He arrived late in the morning to find Ed still in bed. He was received by June, who explained that Ed wasn't feeling the best. Richardson expected to leave without paying his respects, but Ed made the effort to get up and greet him.

'He was in shorts and his dressing gown fell off because he was sitting down and I noticed he had these enormous legs. I had never seen legs like that. I am sure Colin Meads has legs like that but Ed's legs . . . I thought, "God they took him to the top of Everest" and I am not surprised he was picked, because those legs would have carried you anywhere. These were the legs of an 80-year-old-plus man, but they were noticeable.'

When Richardson's visit came to an end, Ed got up to farewell him. 'From their lounge you had to go up about three steps to reach the front door. It was very steep and Ed couldn't make it up those steps. He faltered at the bottom, so June came and said goodbye to me and that was it.'

Invitations to events around the world regularly turned up in the mail. June was always relieved when Ed showed no desire to accept them. He said he didn't spend much time thinking about the past. The contrast between the gangly powerhouse on Everest and the tired and frail man he had become when he was nearly 90 was depressing. Boredom lurked always in the background. June and Ed filled their days with the routine activities with which most old couples occupy themselves—he had a huge appetite for TV sport, and they went for walks together.

Weighed down with honours, with illness and with years, Ed's thoughts naturally turned to his inevitable end. 'I don't spend a lot of time thinking about dying,' he told the *Listener*, 'but I like to think that, if it did occur, I would die peacefully and not make too much of a fuss about it.'

CHAPTER 17
DEATH AND LEGACY

I have no formal religious beliefs yet feel that this astonishingly complicated Universe did not happen purely by chance but that some Universal Intelligence played a dominant role. I request that on my death there should not be an elaborate ceremony but that it be a simple and cheerful occasion which includes the singing of one of my favourite hymns 'How Great Thou Art'.

—From Ed's will

Ed knew he was dying. He was 88 years old. The health problems of the past few years had gained a momentum that could not be stopped. 'He worked out what was happening and was gradually pulling back,' says Mark Sainsbury.

To a few special friends he made a point of saying goodbye—without, of course, acknowledging that that was what he was doing. 'We all knew he was getting sick,' says Sainsbury, who was a regular visitor in Ed's last years. 'I was going back to Wellington for Christmas and called to see him and he was in bed. It was lovely because he started talking about the times we had been together. And the fun we had. You knew.'

Sainsbury decided to ring Tom Scott. He put Ed on the phone.

'We've had a lot of fun, Tom,' said Ed. 'We've had a lot of laughs together.'

'Yes we have, Ed.'

Sainsbury concludes, 'We both knew what the conversation was.'

Ed did his stoical octogenarian best not to acknowledge ill health or pain. The last time he saw Scott and his partner Averil Mawhinney, Averil took champagne to share. Ed surprised the couple by making a rare acknowledgement of his condition, saying, 'I'm not too good, Averil.'

'I visited him when he was bedridden,' says John Hillary. 'I still have bees, so I had made up some stickers and printed them off and I made him a pot of honey. I don't know if he ever ate it or not. I just told him about the memories and how much he meant to me. That's all.'

In some ways, Ed's death was the biggest media event of his life—certainly the biggest since Everest. Broadcaster Paul Holmes had approached June about the possibility of what they both knew—but neither admitted to the other—would be an exit interview. June was polite but firm in declining.

Sainsbury also considered the possibility but decided against it. 'Do you sit him down for the last interview?' says Sainsbury. 'I didn't have—not just the heart . . . One side of you wanted to do it; but you're doing it more for yourself than him, and especially for TV because he is starting to get slower.' And, as Sainsbury had noted earlier, people had been conducting legacy interviews for decades by the time he died, not knowing that he would live for nearly 90 years.

After a fall at home, Ed was admitted to Auckland Hospital under the cover name Vincent Stardust, which amused him greatly. He died there alone on 11 January 2008. His quiet end set off a tidal wave of activity and reaction that would last for weeks. Other fallout from Ed's death would continue for years.

That day, Sainsbury was driving from Wellington to Auckland, where he planned to have dinner with Ed that night. For much of the time his cellphone was out of range. 'Once it got back in range,' says Sainsbury, 'there were all these missed calls—Helen Clark, June Hillary, the office—I knew straight away. I rang June, and she said, "I'm not doing anything till you and Tom get here." We knew [Ed's death] would become a circus so we said we would give them a hand managing it. Then we did a [*Close-Up* TV] special that night. All this stuff was going on. It was almost an Ed response— you had stuff to do and you did it.'

There was never any doubt the greatest living New Zealander would have a state funeral, although Sarah says she for one did not expect it. The event might not have been a circus, but it was certainly a major production. Right from the start, it was unlike any funeral most people will ever experience.

The Very Reverend Ross Bay, dean of the Anglican Holy Trinity Cathedral in Parnell, engaged the funeral director. Unusually, in the early stages all dealings concerning details of the funeral were between the funeral directors, the Department of Internal Affairs and the cathedral. June was brought into the picture late in the day and expressed a wish, more optimistic than likely, that the arrangements would be kept as normal as possible. She had a meeting with the funeral director two days later and three days after that there was another meeting involving June, the funeral director, the dean, the Bishop of Auckland, Internal Affairs and Helen Clark.

So complicated were the arrangements—and so far were the distances that many elderly mourners would have to travel—that the funeral did not take place until a full eleven days after Ed's death. The surviving 1953 Everest team members and wives—Alf Gregory, George Lowe, Michael Westmacott and George Band— plus Jan Morris were invited as special guests. The mountaineers were also invited to receptions hosted by the governor-general, and what George Band called a 'mountaineers' farewell organised by the New Zealand Alpine Club, at which a dozen of his friends recalled facets of Sir Edmund's varied life'. Many other great figures from New Zealand mountaineering and adventuring attended, including Ed's critic Norm Hardie, June's ally Jim Wilson, and Ed's protégé Graeme Dingle.

Family divisions were clear to see as the bereaved made their way into the cathedral for the service. June, who, in a touching gesture patted Ed's casket affectionately before she took her seat, was accompanied by Helen Clark. They were followed by Sarah, who sat on the other side of the prime minister from June. Peter and his family sat two rows back.

People and relics from Ed's career were poignantly deployed throughout. The start of the service was marked by ringing the bell from the *Endeavour*—the ship that carried Ed and his team to the South Pole on the Trans-Antarctic Expedition. Four grandchildren took part. Sarah's son Arthur Boyer read an excerpt from Louise's *A Yak for Christmas*. Sarah and Peter shared memories, with glancing mentions of June.

Among the most moving tributes were those from Sherpas, who attended in large numbers. Ang Rita Tshering Sherpa said, 'His loss for us is bigger and heavier than Mt Everest.' Tenzing Norgay's son, Norbu Tenzing Norgay, said, 'When Sherpas heard the news of his death the grief spiralled into mourning only comparable to the loss of a parent. From every monastery in the Mt Everest region, to Sherpa homes and schoolchildren in the Khumbu, [people] gathered by the thousands to light butter lamps and pray for his soul and reincarnation.'

For others who loved Ed, it was not necessarily the funeral they would have chosen. 'Mostly it was too political,' says Ed's nephew

John, 'but there was a time when it was just the cousins—that was really good. The thing that I couldn't believe seeing was when we were on the bus. There were all these people standing on the side of the road. It was overwhelming. I thought if Ed could see that—his own people. That went through my mind. He was a good guy.'

As the cortege left the cathedral, people lined the streets on the way to the crematorium, many rushing forward to throw flowers on the hearse.

Peter and Sarah's feelings were mixed. They were more conscious than ever that their father in a very real sense did not belong to them. The evidence was on either side of the road. He was a public image, almost a creation of the national consciousness, rather than a man who could put his arms around them and shut out the world. He belonged to that world, not to them.

'We didn't get a funeral,' says Peter, 'because it was a media performance. It was a state funeral, it was a huge honour, but there was never a time for the family to mourn or come to terms with things.' He notes that, whereas after most funerals the mourners are invited to the deceased's or another relative's house, 'we had to go back to Government House. A few weeks later we were at [a special ceremony to farewell Ed at] Queen Elizabeth's place at Windsor Castle. You know, it's all fantastic and extraordinary; but there were 24 cameras in the cathedral. None of that is what you normally have in a situation like that.'

Peter and Sarah grinned and bore it. This is how it had been all through their lives, sharing their father with the rest of the country and sometimes the whole world. 'It was a really wonderful thing, but it wasn't a lot about us,' says Sarah. 'We were greatly honoured by it—it was amazing, but it did build up a lot of stress. For most families, there is an opportunity for the private family, just being together, to deal with the whole thing. "Grieving" isn't even the

right word. When someone is 88 and you know there is going to
be a death, that is reality.'

The most that could be dragged up in the way of public controversy over the arrangements for Ed's funeral was high dudgeon
generated in some quarters over the failure of any member of the
royal family—preferably the Queen, but not necessarily—to turn
up. The normally sane *Sunday Star-Times* led the demented charge.
'Buckingham Palace has, at a stroke, infuriated all of New Zealand
and turned mild monarchists into red-hot anti-royalists,' it tried to
thunder.

> As PR botches go, it's epoch-making and hilarious. But as an insult to this
> country and its deepest values, it is unforgivable . . . Edmund and Elizabeth's
> twosome was for many monarchists a kind of symbol of the close bonds be-
> tween their countries. The fact that she can't be bothered even to send a
> minor princeling or pint-sized princess to farewell him should tell even them
> that these bonds are broken.

This was a view based at least partly on a misunderstanding of
the protocol that surrounds such an occasion. 'The Queen never
goes to funerals, except for close relatives and very close friends,' says
Ken Richardson. 'It's always been a rule that the monarch doesn't go.
I think she made one exception when it was Winston Churchill—he
was her first prime minister and he was a hero. I went to see Ed lying
in state and saw [journalist] Barry Soper in a tent waiting for a feed
for Sky. "What do you think about this hoo-ha over the Queen?" he
said. I said it was a load of nonsense. The Prince of Wales came to
[Prime Minister Norman] Kirk's funeral in 1974 and Prince William
came over to see the Christchurch earthquake. But, I said, Ed is not
in that category—he has no constitutional connection and, quite
frankly, I thought it was a beat-up story.'

And besides, the Queen, along with her daughter Princess
Anne and Sophie Countess of Wessex, did farewell her Knight of

the Garter in a special ceremony in St George's Chapel, Windsor Castle, in April. This was attended by Hillary family members, as well as Helen Clark, and some 650 others, including many expatriate New Zealanders, who listened to the service relayed outside. The ceremony included the 'laying up' of Ed's Knight of the Garter banner, which is returned to the family when a knight dies.

Afterwards, according to Ken Richardson, 'Elizabeth the Second pulled the stops out and had the whole family for lunch. The present New Zealand High Commissioner, Derek Leask, had just arrived to take over that post and—bingo!—the Hillarys are going to be there. The Brits must have listened to the criticism because they had the service of taking down the banner, which normally the Queen wouldn't possibly attend. The add-on, which is not normal, was they were all invited to the castle up the hill for lunch with the Queen. That was a dedicated lunch for Ed Hillary.'

Despite reports that Ed's ashes would be scattered on top of Everest—or kept in a small shrine to one side—they were scattered on Auckland's Waitemata Harbour in accordance with his wishes.

Meanwhile grief postponed was grief denied for Peter and Sarah. 'I felt when I finally had real time to myself it was with an old climbing buddy and we went in June to climb Mt McKinley in Alaska,' says Peter. 'Roddy McKenzie is an old friend so we could really talk about it, because his father had died. That was in some ways the first time I really felt I had a bit of a chance to go through the grieving process.'

'I nearly had a complete breakdown after the funeral,' says Sarah, 'We were meant to be doing something and Ed died, and my friend who I was [planning to go] travelling with came over. We had gone through the whole thing with the funeral. I had to cancel air tickets and I was really tired and then we had to prove we'd had a funeral.

And I think I just burst into tears. I couldn't cope.' Sarah must have encountered the only airline employee in New Zealand who did not know Ed Hillary had died.

Sarah and Peter both miss Ed for the same reasons any children miss a father. 'I miss the fact he knows all that stuff,' says Sarah. 'He's the only person you could talk to about certain things. You know how there is that person in your life.'

'There's things that no one else would understand,' says Peter. 'I spent a lot of wonderful times out on expeditions with him, up there building a little school or reroofing something or putting a wild bridge across a gorge—they were just astounding experiences. It was lovely to see the respect that so many people had for him in all walks of life. I remember when a couple of beekeepers came to see him and they just chatted and chatted, drank tea. And similarly, in a little village in the Himalayas, with the simple village farming folk, you can just tell he is enjoying being in their company.'

John Hillary feels it's hard to miss someone who had what Ed did. 'He had a great life. He said that. He had two great wives. He had a fantastic time. I don't think it is a case of missing people. He had a rich life, but then his time had come.'

Even Mark Sainsbury, who co-anchored the funeral coverage of his friend's funeral, found his grief was delayed by the turmoil of the days after Ed's death. 'And then I realised I couldn't pop around to see him like I used to do all the time. It was probably a month before I cried thinking about Ed, because I was doing all this stuff.'

Friends say June—having been through the most public of griefs, involving considerable embarrassments—only began to get over Ed's death three years after the event and thanks to the passage of time.

The first public embarrassment was Ed's will, which appeared in the media before Sarah had seen it. 'I was so upset,' says Sarah. 'It was awful.'

The will was like Ed himself—business-like, direct, thoughtful and with half an eye on posterity. Unusually for a New Zealander, public figure or otherwise, he included a testament in the document, affecting for the plainness of its language and, predictably, drumming up support for his favourite charity.

'I declare that I have had a full life with much happiness and a share of sadness. I have little cause for complaint. If, however, some people in New Zealand feel I have made some contribution to the prestige of my country then they could best demonstrate this by continuing modest support to the Himalayan people I have worked with for so many years.'

The estate was not huge. Ed had never shown interest in acquiring much in the way of wealth, though a modest amount had come his way. Peter, Sarah and the grandchildren each received sums of money. June got the largest share.

'Ed made sure June was comfortable,' says Murray Jones, 'and in law in New Zealand he could have left the whole lot to her, but he didn't do that and June didn't contest that.'

No one was gauche enough to contest Ed's will. 'A lot of people,' says Sarah, 'have said to us: "We contested our parent's will, but it's not on the front page." A lot of people have disagreements, especially after such a stressful funeral that we had.'

'Well, we didn't contest the will,' says Peter.

Peter was concerned early on to maintain control over the Ed Hillary intellectual property. 'That's something Ed would never have thought about,' says Jones. However, Ed's name is extremely potent, especially in areas with which he himself had commercial associations, such as outdoor pursuits. Anyone who put their mind to it could come up with numerous ways to exploit the intellectual property. The Hillary brand could make other people very wealthy if they had access to it, and could seriously damage Ed's memory if it were misused.

Peter and Sarah now own the rights to the Hillary name, being the two shareholders in Ed Hillary IP Ltd, established in 2011. Anyone wanting to use Ed Hillary intellectual property or naming rights must apply to the company. If the company had been in existence three years earlier, a pizza chain would almost certainly not have been able to produce an ad that appeared in 2008 showing an animated skeletal Ed dancing in a graveyard—a piece of promotional poor taste that appalled almost everyone.

Peter has also looked into the possibility of reviving Hillary Honey and has applied to register a trademark.

The public conversation over the will did not make it easy for anyone to get through their grief. 'I was very upset,' says Sarah. 'But it was months and months after that I went through this roller-coaster of emotions, thinking about the past. Peter and I sorted through various material that we'd been left—and you look at your past. There are old things our parents had when we were very young, wedding presents, so it's a very up and down experience.'

'It's very complicated,' says Peter. 'I think for me too—it sort of reintroduces Dad's passing, then Mum comes back into your mind.'

Peter and Sarah's mourning was also muddied by a dispute with Auckland Museum that began in the year of Ed's death. Ed had a huge amount of archival material stored in his house—documents, private and public, dating back many decades and relating to every area of his life. His will gave ownership of 'my personal papers, diaries, maps, colour slides, photographs and other written and illustrative material relating to my life and adventures' to Auckland Museum 'with the proviso that [Sarah and Peter] shall have ready access to and the right to publish such material if they think fit'. It included a caveat that 'no other person nor any corporate body may publish any such material without the agreement of my children'.

There was some ambiguity there—did 'any corporate body' mean 'any *other* corporate body' besides the museum, or did it mean 'any corporate body' including the museum? Peter and Sarah, aware that many precious early family items were included in the archive, were sure that the phrase was meant to include the museum.

The museum was so sure of its rights to this material that it announced an exhibition, which Sarah only found out about when she saw it advertised. The blame for the debacle was laid squarely at the feet of the museum's director, Vanda Vitali, who had been in the job for just a year.

'She came from more of an exhibition background,' says Sarah, who knows a thing or two about how cultural institutions work. 'She didn't seem to be aware about having good relationships with the family of a collection and how much you can gain from that.'

Peter and Sarah were seen by some as behaving in a privileged and proprietorial way in this affair, but they weren't the only ones to take offence at the Vitali way of doing things. 'Don't just focus on us,' says Peter. There were also matters of concern raised by war veterans.

There were good reasons to work closely with the children. 'Peter knows so much about Ed's life,' says Sarah. 'We know a lot of things about the materials and, if you cut us out, how are you going to find that out?'

'I had half Ed's climbing gear, because I used it,' says Peter.

'The material hadn't even been finalised,' says Sarah, 'so we contacted them and said, "Why didn't you even send us an email about this before you advertised?" and we got a legal letter effectively saying, "We are sorry you are upset but we can do whatever we like." The reason we were so upset was because [the material] contained all our family photos, which hadn't been separated out at that time. I think that was something that the general person could relate to—that no one would want that to happen.'

Suddenly, two of the country's most venerated institutions— Auckland Museum and the Hillary family—were at loggerheads. Peter and Sarah instituted legal proceedings. But before it got to court Prime Minister John Key, who had taken over from Helen Clark in the interim, stepped in.

'The important thing is we have a solution based on trust and goodwill and it respects Sir Ed's wishes and his enormous reputation,' was Key's view. Eventually the Hillarys and the museum were able to achieve a resolution by mediation. It took more than a year to resolve, but eventually was settled in a deed of agreement signed on 19 July 2009.

Simply put, the agreement allowed Sarah and Peter the right to their father's material and to allow others access to that material. The museum had been unwilling to grant them this previously. Peter and Sarah wanted access—among other reasons, because no one knew exactly what was in the archive. So the agreement included the appointment of an archivist to catalogue the material. This would provide a clear basis for deciding how it should be handled.

'All that stuff is over now,' says Peter, 'and we just want a peaceful time. We have a great relationship with the museum now.'

And what would Ed have said?

'He would be furious,' says Peter.

'He would hate it,' adds Sarah.

'Frankly it is all unnecessary. The whole business. I can say for Sarah and I, it's been a bloody nightmare.'

Sarah believes he would have marched to the museum and taken all the things back. 'He would've,' agrees Peter. 'He would've taken it all back. They might have said you have given it, but he wouldn't have stood for it. And all of this stuff with June, he would have hated it. And, quite frankly, I have hated it. We have all hated it.'

As if to complete the physical dismantling of Ed's life—his ashes on the Waitemata, his papers in the museum—his house was bought and removed to Sir Edmund Hillary Collegiate, a school originally founded by Ed and located in southeastern Auckland at Otara. Ed's will directed the house be sold—after giving June reasonable time to find another home—in part to fund bequests to his children and grandchildren.

'The nicest thing,' says Hilary Carlisle, 'was all our generation—Peter, Sarah, and myself—getting together for the last time at the Hillary house before it was sold. It was Easter weekend, we had a barbecue and some drinks. It was a gorgeous day. We all roamed around the house and we talked about each of our adventures in the house as kids. Peter and Sarah showed us all the cupboards they used to hide in.'

The purchaser was Ed and June's neighbour, Terry Jarvis, who wanted to acquire the land but not the building and announced he would probably demolish it. At this point interested parties began looking for a way to save one of the country's most historic homes. After all, it was here where Ed had lived for nearly 60 years and where some of his greatest exploits had been planned.

Eventually it was decided to move the house to the school, where it would be converted into the Sir Edmund Hillary Leadership Centre. It was the sort of solution Ed himself would have come up with, especially when Jarvis offered to share with the government the cost of cutting up and removing the house.

Another option floated to secure the house's future was to incorporate it somehow into Auckland Museum but 'the museum owns no land and has no ability to accept the donation of a house,' Vitali said at the time.

And as bitter, embarrassing and emotionally exhausting as the events of Ed's death and the aftermath had been, they were as nothing compared to the affair of the watches.

CHAPTER 18
THE WATCH THAT BECAME A TIME BOMB

On 29 May 1953 the explorers Sir Edmund Hillary and Sherpa Tenzing Norgay with their Oyster took their first steps on the roof of the world . . . The same year, in a tribute to his historic feat, Rolex officially launched the Explorer model.
—Rolex promotional material

Ed and Rolex had a close association over the years: Ed was perceived as an ideal figure to endorse the company's extremely expensive, upmarket timepieces. His image still appears on the company's website, along with those of other great adventurers.

He was photographed for a Rolex ad with Reinhold Messner, the first person to summit Everest without oxygen. Messner was considerably shorter than Ed, so for the full-length photo a hole was dug in the snow to bring them closer together in height—Ed being brought down to Messner's level presumably because there was no way Messner could come up to his.

Ed owned many watches, but the pearl in his collection was the Rolex Oyster Perpetual presented to him after Everest. Rolex enthusiasts are the trainspotters of horology, obsessing over the tiniest details of the timepieces in a way that would have left Ed nonplussed. He was the opposite—not one to fetishise possessions, he regarded a Rolex as something you used to tell the time, just as an expedition blazer was an item of clothing to wear. Every member of the 1953 Everest expedition had been supplied with a Rolex Oyster; and for him, it was just a watch.

The question of which timepiece was the first watch to get to the top of Mt Everest is the 'Did Mallory get there first?' of chronometry. As with that question, there is really no doubt. The watch Ed actually wore on the climb was one produced by the English watchmakers, Smiths. 'I carried your watch to the summit. It worked perfectly,' Ed said in ads for that company.

He also endorsed Rolex, but without saying he wore a Rolex on the climb: 'Its accuracy is all one could desire and it has run continuously without winding ever since I put it on some nine months ago . . . I count your watch amongst my most treasured possessions.'

Ed did, however, reportedly wear the Rolex when he tractored to the South Pole in 1958. And it was the Rolex that provided a significant final chapter in the deteriorating relationship between Ed's widow and his children. Auckland's independent news-paper *The Independent* called it 'The Rolex that became Hillary's Timebomb'. June's decision to sell Ed's watches—and Peter and Sarah's determination that she should not—brought the feud to the public's attention. The general reaction was a mixture of bemuse-ment and disappointment.

Families frequently fall out over relatively inconsequential things. The Hillarys had had disagreements before, of course, over the Himalayan Trust and numerous other matters of import. But the watches were different. Perhaps passions were higher than normal because a watch is something a son usually inherits from his father.

June decided to auction the watches to raise funds for the Himalayan Trust.

'I wouldn't for a second believe June Hillary would sell those for herself,' says Mark Sainsbury. 'She said, "I was always selling them to raise money for the Trust."'

'I was phoned by Radio New Zealand and they told me they were for sale,' says Sarah. 'We had heard earlier on. Someone had alerted [Peter's wife] Yvonne that they'd heard the Everest watch was going up for sale.'

Peter was in no doubt that the watches belonged to him. He believed the watches had been left to Sarah and him. He believes it was pretty outrageous. 'Second marriages do bring in all sorts of issues. But I think it was unfortunate that June chose not to talk— she just felt she would do what she wanted to do and you just go "That's extraordinary", really. Ed Hillary was my father, but he was a very special man; he did some very special things. It wasn't just a family issue. It wasn't just for Sarah and I to say these things belong to us and we'll do with them as we wish.'

June was deeply hurt by suggestions that she was selling the watches for her own benefit. The whole watch saga 'was very sad, especially for my mother,' says Hilary Carlisle. 'It was very stressful and in the end you adopted the position where you didn't say anything because it was too difficult. But Mum was a bit razzed up about it. The whole watches thing would not have happened if communication was working before.'

The affair quickly went messily public. One newspaper had front-page photos of June and Peter, laid out going head to head. 'It wasn't public or anyone's business,' says Sarah, 'but we couldn't stop it. There are two sides of the coin to being well known.'

Somehow the infighting at the Himalayan Trust, where June at this point still held sway, appeared to get mixed up in it all. 'I had been proposing that Peter become a member of the Himalayan Trust,' says Mike Gill, 'and I received a letter of expulsion from the Himalayan Trust the same day. By absolute chance I was at home—the courier came to the door and handed me a letter and it was a very formal letter signed by June, Lady Hillary, Jim Wilson, Murray Jones and all the family. It was pretty weird, but on exactly the same day, in the paper appeared this headline saying, "Hillary watches to be sold at auction in Geneva". So the media called Peter [about the watches] and said, "What's this?" He said, "I've never heard of this. It's news to me." And he said "Oh, that's interesting, because one of Ed's friends has been expelled by the Himalayan Trust this morning." So the media came to me and they loved it. I was the lead interview on television that night.'

In Geneva, the watches were to be offered as part of a sale of 'Important Modern and Vintage Timepieces' by Antiquorum, which describes itself as the world's premier watch auctioneer. Watch enthusiast Ben Clymer was beside himself as he described the offering on his blog, Hodinkee.

The Hillary collection includes six lots, all of which come with signed certificates of authenticity from Lady Hillary, and each watch represents a milestone in this man's life.

Lot 615: A Seiko Quartz number presented to Hillary in 1988 at the World Expo.

Lot 616: A two-tone Rolex Oyster Quartz purchased by Hillary himself in 1992 to celebrate the 40th anniversary of his attempt to climb Cho Oyu from the Nepal side . . . Original sales receipt included that shows it was sold to Edmund Hillary.

Lot 617: 18k yellow gold Rolex Oyster. Date purchased by Hillary on the 50th anniversary of the day he reached the peak of Everest. Comes with proof it was sold to him on that date.

Lot 618: Rolex Explorer Ref 1016 purchased by Hillary in 1972 to celebrate the 20th anniversary of his attempt to scale Cho Oyu from the Nepal side.

This watch is incredibly important as it is Hillary's own Explorer, the watch that was named for him and his adventures on Mount Everest.

Lot 619: Rolex Explorer II Ref 1655 purchased by Hillary in 1973 to celebrate 20th anniversary of the day he reached the summit of Everest. Having purchased the Explorer I the year earlier, it only made sense for him to buy the just released Explorer II to celebrate this occasion. Estimate is $10,000–$15,000 . . .

Lot 620: Incredibly important Rolex Ref 6084 presented to Sir Edmund Hillary by Rolex of India immediately after his ascent of Mt. Everest in 1953. We know it was given to him after he returned from Everest because of the 'Sir' engraved on the caseback—he received knighthood on June 6th, 1953, just a week after descending. He returned to Europe from Nepal via Calcutta, which is where he likely received this watch. He later wore this timepiece on his next great adventure, the Commonwealth Trans-Antarctic Expedition of 1955–1958.

But before anyone could be bidding on anything, Peter and Sarah had gone to the High Court in Auckland and gained an injunction which effectively prevented the sale going ahead.

The Ministry for Culture and Heritage expressed the view that at least Lot 620 might be subject to the provisions of the Protected Objects Act, which would have prevented it leaving New Zealand. It's interesting, of course, to consider what it says about New Zealand's sense of self that a Swiss item worn on a British expedition in an Asian country should be a protected object.

In an unlikely, but not impossible scenario, June could have been prosecuted for allowing that to happen. Over several days, she tried to get the watches withdrawn from sale.

Antiquorum was not impressed. 'I've never heard of an item of personal property, actually belonging to a man, being claimed as heritage for a country,' said managing director Julien Schaerer, who can't have spent much time in European museums and art galleries. There were mutterings about a financial penalty for June if the watches were withdrawn from sale. 'It's a simple equation,' said Schaerer. 'We had huge amounts of interest in the watches, and already had a lot of registered bidders.'

The High Court took some time considering to whom Ed had left the watches. But the relevant clause in the will seems unambiguously to favour Peter and Sarah as owners of the watches. The clause states that after the bequests have been made and the house and other specified items disposed of, 'the balance of my residuary estate' should be divided 'between such of my children Peter Edmund Hillary and Sarah Louise Hillary as shall survive me and if both shall survive me then in equal shares'.

Granting his injunction in November 2010, Justice Geoffrey Venning said, according to the NZPA report, 'Lady Hillary thought the watches had been given to her by Sir Ed and she had not heard from Peter or Sarah Hillary about the watches since Sir Ed died in January, 2008.' He said it was '"perhaps surprising" Lady Hillary made the decision to sell the watches without consulting Peter or Sarah Hillary', although he added that this observation was not intended as a criticism of June. He had also been at pains to note that once Peter and Sarah's concerns about the sale of the watches had been raised, June took steps to resolve the matter and all concerned had 'responsibly and reasonably agreed on a process to resolve the issue between them'.

Earlier in November, Otago Museum opened a small display of items recently donated by June Hillary. The seventeen pieces of memorabilia included the camera Ed used to photograph Tenzing on Everest, rock shards from the mountain, a 'Hillary's Honey' honey pot, a luggage tag, his first and last passports and other artefacts. Peter said he had only learnt about the gift when he read about it in the newspaper and was 'deeply saddened' that June had given away the items without consulting the family. The camera was among several items that 'accompanied me to the summit of Everest' that Ed's will left to June to 'use as she thinks fit including their sale if she so desires'.

The watches took some time to get home. Their return was finally effected by Rolex enthusiast Philipp Stahl, who had connections with all the relevant parties. As he wrote on his website in June 2011:

> Now some 6 months later, Hillary's collection was still in [Antiquorum's] vault. Today we finally reached agreement in sorting out the loss AQ claimed they had by not auctioning the Hillary collection. I had a long debate with Evan & Julien that started when I was in Geneva last time, with Peter Hillary & Jamling Tenzing Norgay for our HTE project. Several meetings finally made it happen that today the whole collection is free again to travel back to NZ where the historical Rolex Bosecks will be displayed soon in the Auckland museum that has a permanent exhibition on Sir Edmund Hillary.

The intended Lot 620—the 'Everest Rolex' that had been presented to Ed by Bosecks, Rolex's retailer in India—is now in Auckland Museum. 'Sarah and I have given it to the museum, along with a whole lot of other things,' says Peter, 'and I think it is the right place for these very special things to be. I think, rather than me just wearing that watch once a month, it is really better off residing in a public place where the community can also appreciate it. It can be looked after and enjoyed by a lot of people. I know the museum will . . . let me look at it when I want to, so I think that's the right thing to do. Sure, we could have hocked them off and got vast amounts of money; but that was not what that issue was about. It is a special keepsake for the family.'

It was humiliating for June. After the affair was over, she was also interviewed, somewhat to her surprise, by ABC-TV's *Foreign Correspondent* program during the anniversary visit to Khumjung, where Peter was also present. 'An Australian crew there asked for an interview about the Khumjung anniversary and she got caught unawares,' says Mark Sainsbury. 'She can look a bit haughty. And that's why she's particularly gun shy [about being interviewed].'

Asked by *Foreign Correspondent*'s reporter Eric Campbell about the watches, when she expected to be asked only about the Trust's work, June was startled. 'But that's nothing to do with the Himalayan Trust,' June answered. 'Absolutely nothing, except that I wanted to sell them to give the money to the Himalayan Trust. [Peter] didn't like that. Ed gave them to me to do that and I haven't been allowed to do it.'

'Obviously we have to ask about it,' says Campbell.

'But why?'

'Because it's been in the public arena.'

'In Australia?' asks June in apparent disbelief.

'In Australia and obviously in New Zealand.'

June is obviously appalled to learn that this family affair is an international talking point. 'That's disgraceful.'

Asked if he would like to repair the relationship with June, Peter avoids a direct answer. 'You know, I don't wish the Mulgrews any ill. I would like to see them. We were actually very keen that [June's granddaughter] Rebecca [Hayman] stay on the Himalayan Trust council, but that was her decision to go as well.'

'I would really like to see a repair,' says Sarah. 'I'd like everything to calm down. I think we have all got things to contribute and let's just get on with that. I would love that to happen. It would be nice to talk to her when things have calmed down.'

'It was all so unnecessary,' says Peter. 'I am glad it is over and everyone can get on with their lives—that's what we should do and I know that's what our father would want us to do.'

'We just want to go on to a positive future,' says Sarah, 'because there is a whole family. We have known them all for most of our lives. But the thing is: I am not in contact with June at the moment, because it's all been a bit recent and we all need to have some space. I think we just need a bit of a break. But I am looking forward to a nice peaceful future, because it has been bandied around as a family feud. It never really was a family feud, but it was an unfortunate situation. The only way we could stop the watch sale was to go to the court, which was unfortunate. And then it got into the media.'

Mark Sainsbury, who is clearly closer to June than her step-children, isn't sure the relationship can ever come back from the watch debacle. 'I don't know if there ever would be a truce,' says Sainsbury. 'I can see it from Peter Hillary's view as well—suddenly feeling displaced. It's probably always not going to work. But [June's friends] were angry because they said the whole point of selling was for the Trust and never for June Hillary, but she got painted as the greedy widow.'

'I'm very sad about all this stuff that's going on,' says Cath Tizard. 'I know June and Peter Hillary never got on, but the bitterness that seems to have risen is very sad. Every few months we get together and have a gossip. I heard a good deal about this latest row over watches. She, I think, has tried to be discreet about it all; but she's the one who's got the blame publicly for all this. It's her way of protecting Ed Hillary's memory, to be reserved about their relationship.'

Tom Scott thinks peace may reign from now on. 'Maybe now the Trust is in [Peter's] hands and him and June Hillary have given up wrestling. June is 80 now.'

Although the Everest Rolex now resides in Auckland Museum rather than on the wrist of a plutocratic mountaineering enthusiast, it will still be possible for a few people to own a Rolex or two with a Hillary connection, in the form of the Rolex Hillary Tenzing Edition Explorer set, produced with the involvement of Philipp Stahl. According to the website press material:

> The limited Hillary Tenzing Explorer series has been created in close coop-eration with Peter Hillary and Jamling Tenzing Norgay, sons of the famous mountaineers and acclaimed adventurers themselves. 'I am very excited to

participate with Jamling in this unique project,' says Auckland-based Peter Hillary. 'We talked a lot about it during our recent trip to Kilimanjaro and really like the celebration that the Rolex Hillary Tenzing Explorer packages represent [. . .] a great team achieving great heights on Everest.'

The Hillary Tenzing Explorer tribute will be produced in a limited edition series of only 88 packages, consisting of 3 customised Rolex Explorer models and several custom-made items commemorating the successful 1953 ascent. All items will be packed in a handcrafted Everest expedition crate, individually numbered including a signed certificate by Peter Hillary and Jamling Tenzing Norgay.

Potential buyers of the set—costing €28,800 plus VAT—were also offered 'access to an inspiring lecture by Peter Hillary and Jamling Tenzing Norgay in March 2011 in Maastricht, the Netherlands'.

CHAPTER 19
ED OF STATE

Ed was as iconic as a New Zealander can get, and never more so than when he was making self-deprecating fun of his iconic status.

'He hated being called an icon,' says Alexa Johnston. '"What is this?" he would say. "It doesn't mean anything." One day I went around and June told me Ed had said that morning, "I don't want to get out of bed." She had pulled the duvet off and he said, "You can't do that to me—I'm an icon."'

'He ticked all the boxes in terms of the New Zealand psyche,' says Graeme Dingle. 'Big, rugged-looking, apparently humble, not given to talking a lot, no talking about the deeds, being accessible to people.'

The ingenuity. The can-do attitude. The stoicism. The humble origins that gave egalitarian credibility. But he was also the anti-Kiwi who only got where he did by possessing a lot of qualities that New Zealanders lack and in some cases reject—ambitious, a ruthless competitor, an active citizen, happy to give others the benefit of his opinion on matters of public interest. These are other countries' virtues, not New Zealand's.

With his stature came an immunity to criticism, which his son and daughter sometimes struggled with. New Zealand needed Ed to be perfect—and insisted he was, even though Ed himself was forthright about his failings in print and in interviews. He was equally candid about his strengths.

'There is a need in society [for] figures [that] can't be criticised,' says Sarah. 'It makes them feel reassured that there is someone they can believe in or that will do the right thing.'

Sarah and Peter say that even with complete strangers who had never met Ed, any differing view they might have of their father was not allowed to prevail. Everyone made the Ed Hillary they needed, and there was no shifting the image.

'He was a complicated person,' says Peter. 'It's a good thing we illuminate and uplift some ideals. People come up to me all the time and they tell me what the facts are for them about Ed Hillary. There is no point me saying "No, that's not right," because that's what it is for them.'

Tom Scott's youthful experience of the legend was no doubt typical of the experience of many thousands of young people in the 1960s: 'Ed's story meant more to me than any other, growing up in New Zealand,' says Scott. 'I remember reading a *School Friend* magazine that my sister used to get from England and it said, "New Zealand is a mountainous country with fast flowing rivers. The boys play rugby and the girls join marching teams and a New Zealander, Hillary, climbed Mt Everest." I read this in our house in Feilding and thought [. . .] it sounded like the dullest place on earth. And the one thing that made it special at all—the one and only thing . . . Ed was our point of difference. Something magical and heroic and historic had been done by a New Zealander. He was hugely important to us.'

Ed's continuing successes over decades played a large part in making New Zealanders feel they wanted to belong to their country. If it could produce someone like him, maybe it had something going for it.

Fifty years later, after Ed's death, the same sentiment was being expressed in online tributes from ordinary people moved to post comments: 'A New Zealander that all New Zealanders identified with and a New Zealander that all of the world had heard of. A man from a different era when there were still truly dangerous and wonderful adventures to be had,' said one. 'Sir Edmund Hillary, a great man, a hero, a historic figure, a Kiwi,' echoed another. 'I have shared with my students the accomplishments of this man from a small, but strong nation. As I tell them to reach for their dreams, and strive for greatness, his name is always very prevalent in those conversations. He is, and will continue to be, one of the greatest examples of the human spirit.'

'I have a memory of him talking about what he'd been doing in Nepal,' says Alexa Johnston, 'and I remember thinking how lucky we were to have a national hero who was also a good person, hadn't just made a lot of money for himself. He had done exciting things; but he had that core belief that it is worthwhile, if you've got a chance to do something to make other people's lives better, you might as well do it.'

Ed seems to have been genuinely unaware of the magnitude of his celebrity. He once spoke at a dinner at Waikato University attended by a group of retired Americans. Afterwards June mentioned to Ed that some of the men were in tears. 'What did I say?' asked Ed, concerned that he may have inadvertently upset them. 'He didn't realise,' says Johnston, 'that these men were overwhelmed with emotion at speaking to this man they had worshipped all their lives.'

Some hoped a little of Ed's glamour might rub off on them by association. US Secretary of State Hillary Clinton was famously caught out when she hinted that she had been named after Ed. It's possible her parents had heard of the beekeeper before 1947, when she was born; but not likely.

People often wondered how Ed handled fame. In fact, he adapted it to suit his needs. 'I think that he made a deliberate decision in 1953 when he was knighted straight after the expedition,' says Dingle, 'that that was the end of his normal life. He would essentially be a servant of people and he would accept the glory, the glamour; but it came with a huge price. Even in his eighties he was attending functions almost every day and night. There is no way that, if someone wanted a life of their own, they could do that. I think he was bemused by it. My sense is that the realisation of how famous he was grew as he got older.'

He never expected rewards, and so he never lost a little boy's sense of wonder at the good things that came his way as a byproduct of fame.

Dick Blum is a wealthy American who met Ed when Blum was trekking in Nepal in the 1970s. As a result, Blum founded the American Himalayan Foundation. 'It gives huge amounts of money for things like restoring frescoes in Tibetan monasteries and literacy programs for street kids,' says Johnston. When Johnston knew Blum's 60th birthday was coming up, she asked Ed if he was going. 'Alexa, do you know what?' said Ed. 'I can't believe this. Dick said there's three people he wants at his birthday—Jimmy Carter, the Dalai Lama and me.'

'And he burst out laughing.'

Ed also never failed to honour a commitment once it was made, no matter who was offering an alternative. He was invited to lunch with the Queen to celebrate the 50th anniversary of the Everest climb, but declined because he had agreed to be in Nepal on that day. However, he was available the following day for a memorial service.

'The good thing is,' he said, according to Johnston, 'Dick has offered to fly me from Kathmandu to London. He's got a Lear jet. I've never been in a Lear jet—they've got beds and everything.'

He had an innocent's attitude to money, which was once a very New Zealand virtue. Peter Hillary told the story at Ed's funeral of how his father had been rung and invited to do an ad for a breakfast cereal. There was just one problem—Ed didn't like that particular brand of cereal. The agency said that didn't matter—all he needed to do was say the words and get the money. 'Unfortunately, it matters to me,' said Ed.

Of all the honours he received, the most singular was his selection to be the face on the New Zealand five-dollar note. Customarily, living people are not depicted on currency, because of the remote possibility they may—no matter how respected or apparently virtuous—subsequently do something to tarnish their reputations. This was never going to happen with Ed.

In 1953 New Zealand was, as Scott noted, just developing its own identity, and Ed's career played a part in that development. Acting Prime Minister Keith Holyoake, announcing the success on Everest, sounds uncertain as to what country he belongs to: 'I'm able to announce that a news flash has just come through advising us that the New Zealander Hillary has succeeded in conquering Mt Everest. [. . .] Hillary has indeed mounted to the top of the world—and he has put the British race and New Zealand there with him.'

Ed, on his first visit to England, noted that he felt, as many New Zealanders did in those years, right at 'Home'. But he didn't feel that way for long, and he soon became keenly aware of the differences between the two countries. He told Johnston a story about walking along a street in London and being yelled at by someone from a passing car, 'Good on you, Ed. You've done very well for your country.' Back in New Zealand he encountered someone who said 'Good on you, Ed. You've done very well for yourself.'

But Ed didn't do nearly as well for himself as he might have. His lack of interest in material comforts and possessions was a big part of the legend. He certainly made money from his fame, but not nearly as much as he could have if he had knuckled down and taken every promotional opportunity that came his way.

Ed was often described as an ordinary human being, and New Zealand is one of the few countries that rates being ordinary as a cardinal virtue. He was, of course, anything but. He was down-to-earth, which is not the same thing at all. Yet he had some of the trappings of ordinariness, such as keeping his listing in the phone book.

Hilary remembers calls from America in the middle of the night; the caller oblivious to the fact of a time difference between their country and Remuera Road. 'Kids would ring up asking for contributions to their school projects. Ed, when he was there, would talk to them.'

He was accessible to a degree that verged on the brink of self-harm. 'He used to have a page for his diary in his pocket,' says Johnston. 'I was there looking through things at the kitchen table. The phone rang and it was somebody coming to New Zealand and they wanted to bring something for him to sign. They'd always say: "I bet you don't get this very often. I'm only here for a few days." It was happening all the time, of course. He'd get out his diary and say, "Yeah there's a gap at 10.30 on that day. You can come then."'

People often brought five-dollar notes to the house for Ed to sign. The bearers were always ushered in, despite June's frequent protestations: 'You don't have to bring them in, Ed.'

'Oh, I couldn't do that. I couldn't leave them at the front door.'

One national archetype he didn't embody was that of the man alone. He was a very sociable being. As we have seen, mountaineering is a strange mixture of solitary and group activity. All Ed's favourite things involved large groups of people. When Ed invited you to a party, you turned up, says Graeme Dingle. 'Sometimes we would plan expeditions, but it was more a spur of the moment thing. If we decided we were going to do something, we would just do it; and if we had an opinion about something he didn't agree with, he wouldn't take any notice anyway. But usually we would just have parties at the house and everyone would have a great time. There would never be arguments, but there would be heated discussions with people.'

That sociable host is in sharp contrast to the lonely boy taking the long train ride to Auckland Grammar. Lonely people often develop a very gregarious persona. Over his life, Ed developed from being a boy who did things on his own, to being a young man who could meld comfortably into a group of mountain climbers, to being someone who was at home addressing large crowds, to finally being everyone's friend with his name in the phone book so that people could always contact him.

He shaped his celebrity to suit his values, rather than compromising his values to deal with celebrity. Johnston says the representatives from *National Geographic*—which helped sponsor the Auckland Museum show—who travelled to New Zealand were stunned to learn they would be visiting the hero in his own home. And further stunned to find no staff or hangers-on—just Johnston, June and Ed.

'Maybe that's impossible to achieve for famous people now,' says Johnston, 'but he did, and I think you just have to decide that's the kind of life you want to have.'

'It was what he chose,' echoes Dingle. 'The curious thing is that he almost treated total strangers like he would treat his friends and family. There was no distinction, and that brutal honesty was quite evident with his friends and family too.'

Ed never lost the egalitarian spirit that had been bred into him as a child. 'I never thought Ed was ordinary,' says Tom Scott. 'But he didn't expect special treatment. He was as friendly to a stranger as he would have been to a king. [...] He didn't have two Ed Hillarys—a persona for the commoner and one for the king. He was the same with everyone.'

Peter Hillary thinks there was a difference between the private and public Ed Hillary, and that there is nothing exceptional in that: 'I think what Walt Whitman wrote—"We are multitudes"—that's the case of every single person, and with Ed Hillary too. You have got the person on stage; you have the person who is reading their book in the evening, being themselves in their own time.'

'You've got the person who is confident and the person with doubts,' says Sarah. 'I think emotionally he was a bit fragile. That's probably where our mother provided an incredibly important strength in his life.'

Will there ever be another Ed? Graeme Dingle doesn't think so. 'We say Ed is the greatest New Zealander ever. Look at [Maori leader] Sir Apirana Ngata—he made a huge difference to the whole country. He probably made a far greater contribution to New Zealand than Ed Hillary ever did, but we forget about those people. In 50 years, ask young people what they think of Ed Hillary. They will have no idea who he was. Just someone who climbed a mountain somewhere.'

New Zealanders also needed to think of Ed as humble and self-effacing. He was no braggart; but he was very well aware of his achievements: 'Dad would be self-effacing and he would be humble,' says Peter, 'but that doesn't mean you're not as driven as the most driven A-type CEOs that we more typically talk about. I was asked to speak at the Wharton School of Business in Pennsylvania. They were talking about leaders and expeditionary leaders—in particular Scott, Shackleton, Amundsen and Ed Hillary. I was talking about this apparently quite humble side—it is very well known of that type of leader who is an incredibly ruthless and driven leader. Dad's CV doesn't speak of a person who just wandered along and tripped over and said "Oh I got to Mt Everest," and then tripped over and said "Oh I got to the South Pole," tripped over and said, "Blow me, I have got 42 schools—how did that happen?"'

He was also atypical of his countrymen in his willingness to laugh at himself. Tom Scott and Mark Sainsbury became such good friends with Ed at least in part because they made fun of him. 'For most of his life, people were reasonably servile and treated him as this sort of demi-god,' recalls Sainsbury, who, on the other hand, used to tease the great man with: 'Oh Ed—this guy's climbed Everest six times, and you've done it once and lived off it forever.' Sainsbury recalls: 'He quite liked that.' He was enormously amused when Sainsbury, in a mock interview, put it to him that the first thing he did atop Everest was roll Mallory out of the way.

'In the early Himalayan years, he was closest to those who could make him laugh,' says Norm Hardie. 'The clowns. They were Lowe, Mulgrew, then Wilson . . . These men could imitate the questioners who annoyed Ed, or even copy Ed himself.'

Graeme Dingle's sense of humour appears to have been not quite so in tune with Ed's. 'I was just mischievous and played pranks on him. The first night we went camping, we were walking into the Everest area and we were sitting by a campfire. There were a whole lot of Sherpas sitting around the campfire. I thought this looks like a beautiful picture, so I set my camera on the tripod and take a picture of all the faces shining in the firelight. I wanted some smiles so I said to Mike Gill. "Hey, what can I say to make them laugh?"'

Gill told Dingle what to say—the local equivalent of 'my penis won't rest'. The women laughed and Dingle got a happy picture, but Ed was not so amused. A certain reticence in such matters is also in tune with one side of the New Zealand personality.

Ed's old-fashioned courtliness popped up frequently. When Alexa Johnston asked him to sign her personal copy of *An Extra-ordinary Life* he asked, 'Do you mind if I put "Affectionately"?'

Alongside the Himalayan Trust work Ed leaves a legacy, both domestic and global, of inspiration. It's a role he's filled every day since 29 May 1953.

Kevin Biggar, whose polar and transatlantic projects Ed supported, had been inspired by Ed's 'ordinariness', describing it as having 'a really profound effect. You want someone like him to have a third lung or supersize heart. Then you realise the only difference between him and me is that he's done these things.'

That Ed was so obviously mortal put young admirers in a catch–22 situation. If someone ordinary can do amazing things so can you. If you can do amazing things, then you have no excuse not to.

If Ed Hillary hadn't existed, New Zealand would have had to invent him. For the tiny, isolated, sparsely populated country to have a figure of global stature living at home was a source of pride, if not amazement, and contributed enormously to national self-esteem. There was no other candidate with the right mix of qualities. He reflected everything the country wanted to believe about itself. In some cases, as we have seen, those beliefs were accurate. In others, they were not.

BIBLIOGRAPHY

BOOKS

Climbing the Pole: Edmund Hillary and the Trans-Antarctic Expedition 1955–1958, John Thomson, The Erskine Press, 2010

Edmund Hillary: The Life of a Legend, Pat Booth, Moa Beckett, 1993

First Across the Roof of the World, Graeme Dingle and Peter Hillary, Hodder & Stoughton, 1982

From the Ocean to the Sky, Edmund Hillary, Hodder & Stoughton, 1979

High in the Thin Cold Air, Edmund Hillary and Desmond Doig, Hodder & Stoughton, 1962

Himalayan Hospitals: Sir Edmund Hillary's Everest Legacy, Michael Gill, Craig Potton Publishing, 2011

Keep Calm If You Can, Louise Hillary, Hodder & Stoughton, 1964

No Place for Men, Peter Mulgrew, A.H. and A.W. Reed, 1964

Nothing Venture, Nothing Win, Edmund Hillary, Hodder & Stoughton, 1975

Opposite Poles, Doug McKenzie, R. Hale, 1963

Sir Edmund Hillary: An Extraordinary Life, Alexa Johnston, Penguin, 2005

Two Generations, Edmund and Peter Hillary, Hodder & Stoughton, 1984

View from the Summit, Edmund Hillary, Doubleday, 1999

A Yak for Christmas, Louise Hillary, Hodder & Stoughton, 1968

DOCUMENTARIES

HARDtalk, BBC, 1999

Hillary Returns, National Film Unit, 1953

Holmes, TVNZ, 1991

Sir Edmund Hillary, 1919–2008, TVNZ, Roadshow, 2008

A View from the Top: Hillary, TVNZ, Roadshow, 1997

INDEX

INDEX